WHY SOCCER MATTERS

PELÉ

with BRIAN WINTER

WHY SOCCER MATTERS

A CELEBRA BOOK

Celebra
Published by the Penguin Group
Penguin Group (USA) LLC, 375 Hudson Street,
New York, New York 10014

USA | Canada | UK | Ireland | Australia | New Zealand | India | South Africa | China
penguin.com
A Penguin Random House Company

Published by Celebra, a division of Penguin Group (USA) LLC. Previously published in a
Celebra hardcover edition.

First Celebra Trade Paperback Printing, April 2015

CELEBRA TRADE PAPERBACK ISBN: 978-0-451-46875-8

THE LIBRARY OF CONGRESS HAS CATALOGED THE HARDCOVER EDITION OF THIS TITLE AS
FOLLOWS:

Pelé, 1940–
Why soccer matters/Pelé ; with Brian Winter.
p. cm.
ISBN 978-0-451-46844-4 (hardback)
1. Pelé, 1940– 2. Pelé, 1940—Travel. 3. Soccer—History.
4. World Cup (Soccer)—History. 5. Soccer—Social aspects.
6. Soccer players—Brazil—Biography. I. Winter, Brian. II. Title.
GV942.7.P42A3 2014
796.334—dc23   2013043730

Printed in the United States of America
10 9 8 7 6

Set in Adobe Caslon
Designed by Spring Hoteling

For Dona Celeste, with much love

CONTENTS

WHY SOCCER MATTERS

Introduction

I close my eyes, and I can still see my first soccer ball.

Really, it was just a bunch of socks tied together. My friends and I would "borrow" them from our neighbors' clotheslines, and kick our "ball" around for hours at a time. We'd race through the streets, screaming and laughing, battling for hours on end until the sun finally went down. As you might imagine, some people in the neighborhood weren't too happy with us! But we were crazy for soccer, and too poor to afford anything else. Anyhow, the socks always made it back to their rightful owner, perhaps a bit dirtier than we originally found them.

In later years, I'd practice using a grapefruit, or a couple of old dishrags wadded together, or even bits of trash. It wasn't until I was nearly a teenager that we started playing with "real" balls. When I played in my first World Cup, when I was seventeen years old in 1958, we used a simple, stitched leather ball—but even that seems like a relic now. After all, the sport has changed so much. In 1958, Brazilians had to wait for up to a month if they wanted to see newsreel footage in theaters of the championship final between Brazil and the host team, Sweden. By contrast, during the last World Cup, in 2010 in South

Africa, some 3.2 billion people—or about half the planet's population—tuned in live on television or the Internet to watch the final between Spain and the Netherlands. I guess it's no coincidence that the balls players use today are sleek, synthetic, multicolored orbs that are tested in wind tunnels to make sure they spin properly. To me, they look more like alien spaceships than something you'd actually try to kick.

I think about all these changes, and I say to myself: *Man, I'm old!* But I also marvel at how the world has evolved—largely for the better—over the last seven decades. How did a poor black boy from rural Brazil, who grew up kicking wadded-up socks and bits of trash around dusty streets, come to be at the center of a global phenomenon watched by billions of people around the world?

In this book, I try to describe some of the awesome changes and events that made my journey possible. I also talk about how soccer has helped make the world a somewhat better place during my lifetime, by bringing communities together and giving disadvantaged kids like myself a sense of purpose and pride. This isn't a conventional autobiography or memoir—not everything that ever happened to me is contained in these pages. Instead, I've tried to tell the overlapping stories of how I've evolved as a person and a player, and a bit about how soccer and the world evolved as well. I've done so by focusing on five different World Cups, starting with the 1950 Cup that Brazil hosted when I was just a small kid, and ending with the event that Brazil will proudly host once again in 2014. For different reasons, these tournaments have been milestones in my life.

I tell these stories with humility, and with great appreciation for how fortunate I've been. I'm thankful to God, and my family, for their support. I'm thankful for all the people who took the time to help me along the way. And I'm also grateful to soccer, the most beautiful of games, for taking a tiny kid named Edson, and letting him live the life of "Pelé."

EDSON ARANTES DO NASCIMENTO
"PELÉ"
SANTOS, BRAZIL
SEPTEMBER 2013

BRAZIL, 1950

1

―――――

"G*ooooooooooalllllllllll!!!!!!!!*"

We laughed. We screamed. We jumped up and down. All of us, my whole family, gathered in our little house. Just like every other family, all across Brazil.

Three hundred miles away, before a raucous home crowd in Rio de Janeiro, mighty Brazil was battling tiny Uruguay in the final game of the World Cup. Our team was favored. Our moment had come. And in the second minute of the second half, one of our forwards, Friaça, shook off a defender and sent a low, sharply struck ball bouncing toward goal. Past the goalie, and into the net it went.

Brazil 1, Uruguay 0.

It was beautiful—even if we couldn't see it with our own eyes. There was no TV in our small city. In fact, the first broadcasts ever in Brazil were occurring during that very World Cup—but only in Rio. So for us, as for most Brazilians, there was just the radio. Our family had a giant set, square with round knobs and a V-shaped antenna, standing in the corner of our main room, which we were now dancing around madly, whooping and hollering.

I was nine years old, but I will never forget that feeling: the euphoria, the pride, the idea that two of my greatest loves—soccer and Brazil—were now united in victory, the best in the entire world. I remember my mother, her easy smile. And my father, my hero, so restless during those years, so frustrated by his own broken soccer dreams—suddenly very young again, embracing his friends, overcome with happiness.

It would last for exactly nineteen minutes.

I, like millions of other Brazilians, had yet to learn one of life's hard lessons—in life, as in soccer, nothing is certain until the final whistle blows.

Ah, but how could we have known this? We were young people, playing a young game, in a young nation.

Our journey was only beginning.

2

rior to that day—July 16, 1950, a date that every Brazilian remembers, like the death of a loved one—it was hard to imagine anything capable of bringing our country together.

Brazilians were separated by so many things back then—our country's enormous size was one of them. Our little city of Baurú, high on a plateau in the interior of São Paulo state, seemed a world away from the glamorous, beachside capital in Rio where the last game of the World Cup was taking place. Rio was all samba, tropical heat and girls in bikinis—what most outsiders imagine when they think of Brazil. Baurú, by contrast, was so cold on the day of the game that Mom decided to fire up the stove in our kitchen—an extravagance, but one she hoped would help heat up the living room and keep our guests from freezing to death.

If we felt distant from Rio on that day, I can only imagine how my fellow Brazilians in the Amazon, or in the vast Pantanal swamp, or on the rocky, arid *sertão* of the northeast, must have felt. Brazil is bigger than the continental United States, and it felt even bigger back then. This was a time when only the fabulously wealthy could afford cars, and there were hardly any paved roads in Brazil to drive them on anyway. Seeing anything outside your hometown was a distant dream for all but a lucky few; I would be fifteen before I ever saw the ocean, much less a girl in a bikini!

In truth, though, it wasn't just geography that was keeping us apart. Brazil, a bountiful place in many ways, blessed with gold and oil and coffee and a million other gifts, could often seem like two completely different countries. The tycoons and politicians in Rio had their Paris-style mansions, their horse-racing tracks, and their beach vacations. But that year, 1950, when Brazil hosted the World Cup for the first time, roughly half of Brazilians usually didn't get enough to eat. Just one in three knew how to read properly. My brother and sister and I were among the half of the population who usually went barefoot. This inequality was rooted in our politics, our culture, and our history—I was a member of just the third generation of my family born free.

Many years later, after my playing career was over, I met the great Nelson Mandela. Of all the people I've had the privilege of meeting—popes, presidents, kings, Hollywood stars—no one impressed me more. Mandela said: "Pelé, here in South Africa, we have many different people, speaking many different languages. There in Brazil, you have so much wealth, and only one language, Portuguese. So why is your country not rich? Why is your country not united?"

I had no answer for him then, and I have no perfect answer now. But in my life, in my seventy-three years, I have seen progress. And I know when I believe it began.

Yes, people can curse July 16, 1950, all they want. I understand; I've done it myself! But it was, in my mind, the day Brazilians began our long journey down the road to greater unity. The day when our whole country gathered around the radio, celebrated together, and suffered together, as one nation, for the very first time.

The day we began to see the true power of soccer.

3

My earliest memories of soccer are of pickup games on our street, weaving through small brick houses and potholed dirt roads, scoring goals and laughing like crazy between gasps of cold, heavy air. We would play for hours, until our feet hurt, and the sun went down, and our mothers called us back inside. No fancy gear, no expensive jerseys. Just a ball—or something like it. Therein lies much of the beauty of the game.

As for what I did with that ball . . . well, I learned almost everything I know from my father, João Ramos do Nascimento. Like virtually everyone in Brazil, he was known by his nickname—Dondinho.

Dondinho was from a small town in the state of Minas Gerais, literally "General Mines," where much of Brazil's gold was found during colonial times. When Dondinho met my mother, Celeste, he was still performing his mandatory military service. She was in school at the time. They married when she was just fifteen; by sixteen she was pregnant with me. They gave me the name "Edson"—after Thomas Edison, because when I was born in 1940, the electric lightbulb had only recently come to their town. They were so impressed that they wanted to pay homage to its inventor. It turned out they missed a letter—but I've always loved the name anyway.

Dondinho took his soldiering seriously, but soccer was his true passion. He was six feet tall, huge for Brazil, especially in those days, and very skilled with the ball. He had a particular talent for jumping high into the air and scoring goals with his head, something he once did an amazing five times in one game. That probably was—and is—a national record. Years later, people would say, with some exaggeration— the only goal-scoring record in Brazil that doesn't belong to Pelé is held by his own father!

It was no coincidence. I'm certain that Dondinho could have been one of the all-time Brazilian greats. He just never got a chance to prove it.

When I was born, my dad was playing semiprofessional ball in a town in Minas Gerais called Três Corações—"Three Hearts," in English. Truth be told, it wasn't much of a living. While a few elite soccer clubs paid decent salaries back then, the vast majority didn't. So being a soccer player carried a certain stigma—it was like being a dancer, or an artist, or any profession that people pursue out of love, not because there's any real money in it. Our young family drifted from town to town, always in search of the next paycheck. At one point, we spent a whole year living in a hotel—but not quite the luxury kind, let's say. It was, as we later joked, a zero-star resort for soccer players—as well as traveling salesmen and outright bums.

Right before my second birthday, in 1942, it looked like all that sacrifice would finally pay off. Dondinho got what appeared to be his big break. He was called up to play for Atlético Mineiro, the biggest and richest club in all of Minas Gerais. This was, finally, a soccer job that could support all of our family, maybe comfortably. My dad was just twenty-five; he had his whole playing career in front of him. But during his very first match, against São Cristóvão, a team from Rio, disaster struck when Dondinho collided at full speed with an opposing defender named Augusto.

That was not the last we heard of Augusto, who would recover and go on to other things. But it was, sadly, the high point of Dondinho's playing career. He catastrophically damaged his knee—the ligaments, perhaps the meniscus. I say "perhaps" because there were no MRIs back then, no real sports medicine to speak of at all in Brazil, in fact. We didn't really know what was wrong, much less how to treat it. All we knew was to put ice on whatever hurt, elevate it, and hope for the best. Needless to say, Dondinho's knee would never fully heal.

Unable to make it on the field for his second game, Dondinho was quickly cut from the team and sent back home to Três Corações. Thus began the true journeyman years, a period that would see our family constantly struggling to make ends meet.

Even in the best of times, things had been tough—but now Dondinho was around the house a lot, trying to stay off his knee, hoping it would somehow mend and he could go back to Atlético, or someplace similarly lucrative. I do understand why he did this; he thought it was the best path to making a good living for his family. But when he wasn't well enough to play, there was hardly any money coming in, and of course there was no social safety net whatsoever in Brazil during the 1940s. Meanwhile, there were new mouths to feed—my brother and sister, Jair and Maria Lucia, had just come into the world. My father's mother, Dona Ambrosina, also moved in with us—as did my mother's brother, Uncle Jorge.

My siblings and I wore secondhand clothes, sometimes stitched from sacks used to transport wheat. There was no money for shoes. On some days, the only meal Mom could make us was bread with a slice of banana, perhaps supplemented by sacks of rice and beans that Uncle Jorge brought from his job at a general store. Now, this made us lucky compared to a great many Brazilians—I have to say that we never went hungry. Our house was of a decent size, not part of a slum—or *favela*, to use the Brazilian word—by any means. But the roof leaked, and water would soak our floor with every storm. And there was also that constant anxiety, which we all felt, including the kids, about where our next meal would come from. Anybody who has ever been that poor will tell you that uncertainty, that fear, once it enters your bones, it's like a chill that never leaves you. To be honest, I sometimes feel it even today.

Our fortunes improved slightly when we moved to Baurú. Dad got a job working at the Casa Lusitania—the general store, which belonged to the same man who owned the Baurú Athletic Club, or BAC, one of two semiprofessional soccer teams in the city. Dondinho was an errand boy during the week, making and serving coffee, helping deliver mail and such. On weekends, he was BAC's star striker.

On the field, my dad showed glimpses—when healthy—of the brilliance that had once put him so tantalizingly close to the big time. He scored lots of goals, and in 1946 he helped lead BAC to the semi-professional league championship in São Paulo state's interior. He also had a certain charisma, a way of carrying himself with elegance and good cheer despite the bad luck that had befallen his soccer career. Just about everybody in Baurú knew who he was and liked him. I was known wherever I went as Dondinho's son, a title of which I was, and am, very proud. But times were still tight, and I remember thinking even then that it wasn't worth anything to be famous if you couldn't put food on the table.

I guess Dondinho could have sought another skill, another occupation. But soccer can be both generous and cruel. Those who fall under its spell never really escape. And when Dondinho realized that his own dream was falling short, he dedicated himself, heart and soul, to nurturing someone else's.

4

"Ah, so you think you're good, eh?"

I would stare down at my feet, and smile.

"Kick the ball here," he would say, pointing at a spot on the wall of our house.

If I succeeded—and I usually did—he would grin for just a moment, and then abruptly turn serious again.

"Very well! Now do it with your other foot!"

Blam!

"Now with your head!"

Blam!

And so it would go, for hours and hours, sometimes late into the night, just the two of us, me and him. These were soccer fundamentals at their most basic: dribbling, shooting, passing the ball back and forth. We didn't have access to the city's soccer field most of the time, so we used the space available, which consisted of our tiny yard and the street outside, which was called Rubens Arruda Street. Sometimes he'd tell me stories from games he'd played, and show me moves that he'd learned or invented himself. He also talked, on occasion, about his older brother, a midfielder who Dad said was an even better goal scorer than he was, but who died at just twenty-five—another promising career in the Nascimento family that tragically didn't live up to its potential.

Mostly, though, it was just drills, learning the basic skills of the game. Some of the exercises were, in retrospect, pretty funny. One involved tying a ball to a tree limb up high and bouncing it off the top of my head for hours at a time. But that was child's play compared to Dondinho's technique for teaching me how to "head" the ball properly into the goal. He would grab a ball with both his hands and then hit me in the middle of my forehead with it, over and over again. "Don't blink! Don't blink!" he would say. His point was that to really be good, I had to learn to keep my eyes open when the ball hit my head. He even told me that, when I was just sitting around the house, I should pick up a ball and slam it against my head on my own. Which I did—I can't imagine how ridiculous I must have looked! But, obviously, Dondinho thought it was very important—and he was right. It was a lesson that would serve me extremely well later on.

Besides the headers, there were two skills in particular that Dondinho wanted me to focus on: 1) Keeping the ball as close to my body as possible while dribbling, and 2) being able to do everything equally well with both feet.

Why did he emphasize these things? Maybe because of the small spaces we played in—on the streets of Baurú, and in yards and alleys. But also, perhaps, because my dad saw that I was pretty small and scrawny. As an adult, I would grow to be just five feet, seven inches tall; it was clear even then that I was going to be short. So unlike Dondinho, I wouldn't have any natural physical advantages on the soccer field. If I couldn't knock other players out of the way, or jump higher than them, I'd just have to be more skilled. I'd have to learn to make the ball an extension of myself.

Dondinho taught me all these things, it must be said, at considerable risk. My mother, Dona Celeste, *dreaded* the possibility of her oldest son becoming a soccer player. And who could blame her? For Dona Celeste, soccer was this dead-end pursuit, a sure path to poverty. She was a strong woman, always looking out for us. It was often left to her to be the responsible one in a houseful of dreamers. She wanted me to spend my free time studying, so I could make something of myself one day. Then as now, she was like the angel sitting on our shoulders, always encouraging us to do the right, moral, constructive thing. She wanted better lives for all of us. So in those early years, when she caught me playing soccer, she would give me a good verbal lashing. And sometimes much worse!

Despite her well-intentioned efforts, my dad and I couldn't be stopped. What could she do? We both had the sickness. And as time passed, and we kept playing in the little yard, it got to the point where Dona Celeste would just walk outside, put her hands on her hips and heave a resigned sigh:

"Oh, great. Your eldest son! Just don't come complaining to me later when he's starving, instead of studying medicine or law!"

Dondinho would put his arm around her waist, and laugh.

"Don't worry, Celeste. Unless he learns to use his left foot properly, you have nothing to worry about!"

The parent with frustrated dreams of sporting greatness, training a son or daughter to follow in his or her footsteps—it's an old tale, one that is full of peril. Some children resent the burden that comes with these expectations. Other kids, placed under heavy pressure, simply snap. Some of them never kick a ball again.

I never felt any of these things. The simple truth was that I *loved* soccer. I loved the feel of the ball on my foot, the sun on my face, the camaraderie that came with great teamwork, the electricity that ran through my veins when I scored a goal. But most of all, I loved the time that I spent with my dad. During all those long hours we spent practicing, I don't think Dondinho ever thought that I'd be rich or famous, not during those early years, anyway. I think he just loved the damn game—and wanted to pass that love along to his son.

He succeeded. And I have to say, that love has never faded. It's deep inside of me, like religion, or a language you learn from birth. My dad's gone now. But the amazing thing is that, all these years later, I still can't separate my love for soccer from my love for him.

5

Throughout my life, I would have the honor of playing soccer in nearly all of the world's great venues—the Maracanã in Rio, Camp Nou in Barcelona, even Yankee Stadium in New York City. But my very first competitive games were played on the hallowed grounds of "Rubens Arruda Stadium"—which wasn't really a field at all, but the dusty street in front of our house in Baurú. Kids from the neighborhood were my first rivals. We used old shoes for goalposts; the houses were out of bounds (most of the time); and if an errant kick broke a streetlight or window, we'd run like crazy, although everybody usually assumed I was to blame, being known around town as the most soccer-crazy of the whole bunch. I guess that was the one downside of being Dondinho's son!

Our pickup games reflected why I think soccer brings people together like no other single activity. Other sports, like baseball or cricket or American football, require all kinds of expensive equipment or rigidly organized teams. They might have been off-limits to a bunch of poor, unorganized kids in a place like Baurú. But all we needed for soccer was a ball. It could be one-on-one, or eleven-on-eleven, and we were entertained just the same. In our neighborhood, I could run out there pretty much anytime of day and find at least six or ten other kids to play with. Our mothers were nearby, so they could keep an eye on us. But there really wasn't much to worry about in small-town Brazil in the 1940s—there were no cars, hardly any violent crime, and everybody in the community knew one another. So, no matter the time of day, Rubens Arruda Stadium was almost always playing host to a game of some kind, unless the referee—that is, my mom—broke it up.

Another great thing about soccer is that literally anybody can play—you can be small, tall, strong or slight, but as long as you can run and kick, you're perfectly suited to take a soccer field. As a result, our pickup games gathered an incredibly diverse, varied group of kids. Each game was like a little gathering of the United Nations: We had Syrians, Portuguese, Italians, Japanese, and of course many Afro-Brazilians like myself.

In that sense, Baurú was a microcosm of Brazil, which absorbed millions of immigrants from all over the world. It was a true melting pot, just as diverse as—if not more so than—the United States. Many outsiders don't know that São Paulo, even today, has the largest Japanese-descended population of any city outside of Japan. Baurú was two hundred miles from São Paulo, and seemingly one-millionth of the size, but we also absorbed our fair share of immigrants who originally came to work in the coffee plantations just outside our city. My neighbors had last names like Kamazuki, Haddad and Marconi. Soccer made us put aside whatever differences we might have, and I'd go over to their houses afterward to eat yakisoba, kibbe or just plain Brazilian rice and beans. It was a great introduction to the world, and it awakened an early appetite for other cultures—one I would be lucky enough to greatly indulge in coming years.

I was always in a rush to play, so I was usually the one who took charge of dividing up the teams. This was complicated. Why? Well, at the risk of sounding immodest, all those drills with Dondinho were starting to pay off. And that was becoming a problem. My team would win games 12–3, or 20–6. Kids started refusing to play, even those much older than I. So at first, I would try to keep everybody interested by creating lopsided teams, pitting three against seven, for example, and putting myself on the smaller side. When even that wasn't enough, I started playing the first half of the game as the goalie, just to keep the score close, before finally taking up offense toward the end. Playing goalie so often in those years was another decision that would echo throughout my life in the strangest ways, and eventually give me my most famous nickname, the one the world knows me by.

Nicknames are a funny thing in Brazil—almost everybody's got one, and some people have three or four. At that time, I was still known as "Dico"—which my family calls me even today. My brother, Jair, was called "Zoca." And when Zoca and I weren't on the field, we had all kinds of adventures with our friends around town—the railway station was just a few blocks away from our house, and we'd go there to see people arriving from São Paulo and elsewhere—it was our window to the world. On other days, we'd go fish in the Baurú River, right under the railway bridge; we couldn't afford rods or reels, of course, so we'd borrow circular, wood-edged screens, and scoop the fish out that way. On many days, we'd go running with our friends into the forest that surrounded the city, where we'd pick fresh mangoes and plums from the trees and hunt birds, including one species called the tiziu, which briefly became another nickname of mine—because tizius are small, black and fast!

It wasn't all fun and games, of course. Nudged by our family's economic situation, I had started working part-time when I was seven. My uncle Jorge lent me some money and I bought a shoe shine kit—a little box with some brushes inside, and a leather strap for carrying it around. I practiced at first by shining for friends and members of our family, and then when I had the technique down, I went to the train station and shined shoes there. In coming years, I would also work at a shoe factory. For a brief time, I took *pastels*—a delicious, deep-fried Brazilian empanada of sorts, usually stuffed with ground beef or cheese or hearts of palm—that were made by a Syrian woman in our neighborhood and I delivered them to a vendor. He then sold them to passengers on one of the three rail lines that ran through town.

There wasn't much money in any of this—Baurú was poor, like the rest of Brazil. It often seemed like a city of too many shoe shiners, and not enough shoes. But, whatever I earned, I'd dutifully deliver all of it to my mom, who used the money to help buy us food. When times were good, she'd give me a few coins to go see a matinee on Sunday.

There was also school. Here, I'm afraid my performance wasn't quite equal to what I was doing on the field. My enthusiasm for soccer, above all, made me a difficult and often rebellious student. Sometimes I'd just walk out of the classroom and start dribbling a wadded-up piece of paper through the courtyard. Now, my teachers did the best they could—they tried to discipline me by making me kneel on piles of dried beans, or by putting balls of crumpled paper in my mouth to stop me from talking. One teacher would make me stand facing the corner, my arms outstretched, kind of like the Christ the Redeemer statue in Rio. I remember one time I got in huge trouble for crawling under a teacher's desk and looking up her dress.

Over time, I got discouraged by school. There were lots of other things to do, and I'm sorry to say that my attendance became sporadic. This was sadly typical at the time—in the late 1940s, only one in three Brazilian kids went to school at all. Just one in six made it to high school. Still, this was little excuse. I would later regret not having paid more attention as a student, and would go to considerable lengths to make up for it.

For better and for worse, I reserved most of my considerable energy for the soccer field. It was a place where we didn't have to think about poverty, or our parents, or long-ago tragedies. On the field, nobody was rich or poor; it was a place where we could just play. We spent our days talking, breathing, and living the sport. Little did we know, soccer was about to be the backdrop for the biggest thing ever to happen in Brazil.

6

Then as now, there's nothing that gets people everywhere quite as excited as the World Cup. The tournament brings together countries from all over the world every four years for a full month of games, celebrations and pageantry. It's like a huge party where the entire planet is invited. I've been to every one of them for the last fifty-six years, as either a player, fan or designated "ambassador" to the sport of soccer. Based on my experience, I can say with some authority that there's just nothing better. The Olympics are great too, of course, but for my taste there's almost too much going on with all the different events. With the World Cup, it's only soccer—a tournament that builds and builds to an exhilarating climax, the championship game, when the new kings of the world are anointed.

It's such an institution now that it seems like the World Cup has been around forever. But in 1950, when it first came to Brazilian soil, the World Cup was still a relatively new idea—and it was on somewhat shaky ground. The first Cup had been organized only twenty years before, in 1930. A Frenchman named Jules Rimet, who was the president of FIFA, the global soccer body, decided to create a showcase for the ever-more popular sport. His plan was to gather teams every four years, at the midpoint between each Summer Olympics—hoping that it would increase the profile of international teams and also make a contribution to global harmony. Unfortunately, there were only men's teams back then—several more decades would pass until someone had the excellent, long-overdue idea of staging a World Cup for women's teams, as well.

The first few World Cups drew teams from countries as varied as Cuba, Romania and the Dutch East Indies (now Indonesia), as well as already entrenched superpowers like Brazil and Italy. The World Cup grew in prestige and attendance, and by the 1938 edition, held in France, games were playing to big venues packed with tens of thousands of people. But there were several foreboding events at that 1938 Cup, such as when the Austrian team had to withdraw at the last minute—because, three months earlier, their nation had been absorbed into Germany. The German team ended up incorporating several of Austria's best players, but they were eliminated in the first round anyway before a hostile, bottle-throwing crowd in Paris. It was, unfortunately, not the last time that politics would intrude on the soccer field.

When World War II erupted a year later, the World Cup—like so many other things—was put on hold for a long while. The war ended in 1945, but most of Europe was so terribly devastated, and focused on rebuilding its cities and factories, that years would pass before anybody thought it was possible to hold a global soccer tournament again. By 1950, it finally seemed like the Cup was ready to resume—but the organizers needed a host country that hadn't been touched by the war, and could afford to build the stadiums and other infrastructure required. And that's where Brazil came in.

Even after Brazil agreed to host the 1950 Cup, several countries were still too broke to send teams all the way to South America. This was before the age when everyone could travel by jet, and getting to Brazil from Europe could still take thirty hours and require several stops in places like Cape Verde and Recife, on Brazil's northeastern coast. Germany, which was still partitioned and occupied by the Allied powers, was banned from participating. So was Japan. Scotland and Turkey withdrew at the last minute. In the end, only six countries would attend from Europe, which besides South America was the other powerhouse of global soccer. This was too bad for them—but it seemed to be great for Brazil! We were still looking for our first World Cup title, and we thought we were way overdue. With a limited field of competitors, and the games on our home turf, how could we possibly lose?

In Baurú, as elsewhere in Brazil, all of us became consumed by World Cup fever—well, not so much by the Cup itself, but by the absolute certainty that we were about to be crowned the champions of the world. I was only nine, but definitely old enough to get swept up in things. "The Cup is ours!" I remember my dad saying, confidently, again and again, as we all listened to news of the preparations for the tournament on the radio at night. "The Cup is going to be ours, Dico!"

Among my friends, there was talk of celebrations and parades, and arguments over who might get to see the trophy themselves. We played our street games while imagining ourselves as the world champions. In fact, it was pretty amazing how, wherever I went, I couldn't find a single soul who even considered the possibility that Brazil might not win the whole thing.

7

A new energy was taking hold in Brazil, and everybody could feel it. People seemed to have a spring in their step, a desire to impress the world, even in far-flung places like Baurú where the Cup was barely more tangible than a rumor. As such, our little bunch of players on Rubens Arruda Street felt inspired to do something bigger and better. We decided to go beyond just our usual pickup games and organize ourselves into a proper team, like the Brazilian national team, or Dondinho's BAC. We wanted to have all the proper gear—shirts, shorts, shoes and socks. And of course we'd need something better than a wadded-up bunch of socks for a ball.

There was one hitch: We didn't have ten cents among us.

I suggested to the gang that maybe we could raise funds by putting together a collection of soccer stickers. These stickers were all the rage at the time—they were sort of like baseball cards, with each sticker bearing a player's photo and maybe a few statistics as well. So my idea was to get all the kids to pool our stickers together and put them together in an album, focusing on the really popular teams from Rio and

São Paulo, so the collection would be worth more. We'd then find somebody willing to swap the album for a real leather ball.

This plan was quickly accepted, but it still left us many miles short of our ambitious fund-raising goal. One kid nicknamed Zé Porto suggested that we could bridge the difference by selling toasted peanuts at the door to the circus and the movie theater. Ah, a great idea! But where would we get the peanuts? As it turned out, Zé Porto had a ready-made solution for this problem, too. He smiled deviously and suggested that we could just steal some peanuts from one of the warehouses down by the railway.

This idea made some of us really uneasy. I remembered my mom's dire warning that theft was one of the very worst sins. I could sense other boys thinking the exact same thing. But Zé Porto was quite the persuasive fellow. He argued that even if we couldn't get into the warehouse, we could break into one of the train wagons themselves, and, anyway, who would notice if a few bags of peanuts went missing?

"Besides," he added, "anybody who doesn't agree is a big shit!"

Well, we couldn't really argue with that. So down we all went to the train station, walking on eggshells the whole way. As one of the group's unofficial leaders, I was selected as one of the two kids who would actually slip inside the train wagons to get the peanuts. I had my misgivings, but . . . anything for soccer, I guess.

As we slipped into the train wagons, I couldn't shake the mental image of my mom looking over us, arms folded, shaking her head in disapproval and sadness. But it was too late to turn back. We cut the sacks open, and a tidal wave of peanuts came pouring out onto the wood floor. We frantically gathered them up in our pockets, our shirts, and in the rusty old bucket we had brought along for the job. Finally, after what seemed like an eternity, we ran out with our loot and found the rest of the group. We all sprinted home, laughing and shouting with joy—and relief.

We toasted the peanuts and then sold them as planned, using the funds to acquire our shorts. When we realized that shirts were beyond our budget—and that pressing our luck again with the trains was a *really* bad idea—we settled for matching vests instead. That still left us without socks or shoes, but we were too excited by that point to care. At first we called ourselves the *Descalsos*—the "Shoeless Ones"—until we realized there were several other teams in Baurú that had the exact same nickname, for the exact same reason we did.

We became known instead as the Sete de Setembro team, named after the street that intersected mine, which was in turn named for Brazil's independence day—the seventh of September. With our gear now in hand, and a couple of ace players, we began taking ourselves extremely seriously. Before our games, we would file one-by-one onto the field—OK, the street—with great solemnity, just like we'd seen Dad's team do. We scheduled games against other squads in the neighborhood, and we won most of them, sometimes by double digits. I began to make all kinds of crazy moves, bouncing the ball on my head, on my knees. Sometimes, I would laugh hysterically at hapless players from other neighborhoods as I blew past them, on my way to yet another goal.

One evening, Dondinho came home from the general store looking quite upset. When dinner was over, he said he wanted to talk to me—alone.

"I walked by the street where you and your friends were playing today, and I saw what you were doing out there," he said.

My eyes must have lit up. Surely he'd seen me make some great new move?

"I'm furious with you, Dico," he said. "I saw how you were mocking those other boys. You should respect them more. That talent you have? You didn't do a single thing to deserve it. It was God who gave you that talent!

"Those other boys weren't blessed in the same way—so what? That doesn't give you the right to act like you're better than them.

"You're just a boy," he continued gravely, wagging his finger at me. "You haven't done anything yet. Not a thing. When you've accomplished something, one day, then you can celebrate. But even then—you'll do it with humility!"

I was shocked. I remember desperately wanting to go run and hide in my bedroom, which I shared with Zoca. But, as usual with Dondinho, it was superb advice—that conversation would stick with me for many, many years. And as things turned out, it would have been a great warning for the whole of Brazil as well.

8

When the World Cup finally got under way, all of our neighborhood games stopped so that we could pay proper attention to the tournament. And it seemed for a while as if all our breathless excitement had been justified. Brazil won the opening match in Rio in lopsided fashion—a 4–0 slaughter of Mexico, led by two goals from Ademir—a great player from Vasco da Gama who was also known as "Jaw" because of—well, what else?—his prominent chin. The next match was a much more sober affair: a 2–2 tie against Switzerland in the Pacaembu Stadium in São Paulo. But a 2–0 victory over Yugoslavia quickly soothed any nerves, and just like that, Brazil was on to the final round.

From that point on, it was as if a monster had been awakened. Brazil destroyed a pretty good Swedish team by a score of 7–1, led by four goals from "Jaw" alone. Four days later, our team obliterated Spain in similar fashion, racking up a 6–1 win with goals from five different players. The Brazilian team appeared to be skilled and well balanced, with a good defense and a wide range of scoring options on offense. They played to crowds that showered them with chants, confetti, and all the love you'd expect from a hometown audience. And with seemingly no effort, much less suspense, Brazil was now one game away from winning the championship altogether. Maybe Dondinho was right—this Cup would be ours after all.

The matchup was the one everybody had wanted—against Uruguay. A nation of sheep farms and sandy beaches on Brazil's southern border, Uruguay had a population of just over two million people—we had far more folks just in Rio de Janeiro. And they, unlike Brazil, had limped through the final round of play—barely eking out a 2–2 draw with Spain, and needing a goal with just five minutes left to beat Sweden 3–2.

We even had the best possible venue for the game: the brand-new Maracanã Stadium in Rio, which had been built especially for the World Cup. Because of its massive scale and architectural flourishes, it seemed less like a stadium than an imperial palace, financed at lavish cost for the explicit purpose of crowning the home team. The Brazilian government brought in more than ten thousand workers to carry out the construction. As completion neared, the workers would "test" the structure by packing into parts of the stands and celebrating imaginary goals. Luckily, all the pillars and beams held up. When the work was finally finished, two years later, the Maracanã had a capacity of just under two hundred thousand people—making it the biggest stadium in the world, more than forty thousand beyond the runner-up, Hampden Park in Glasgow, Scotland.

Brazilian media and politicians fell all over themselves, seemingly competing to see who could shower the Maracanã—and, by extension, Brazil—with the most praise. "Brazil has now built the biggest and most perfect stadium in the world, dignifying the competence of its people and its evolution in all branches of human activity," the newspaper *A Noite* wrote. "Now, we have a stage of fantastic proportions in which the whole world can admire our prestige and sporting greatness."

If that seems a tad over-the-top, it was nothing compared to the excitement on game day. Carnival-style parades swept through the streets of Rio, singing special songs written to celebrate Brazil's coronation as the best in the world. Many workers took the day off, and filled their houses with beer and sweets in anticipation of the wild party that would surely occur afterward. One newspaper even printed a photo of the team on its front page, with the headline: THESE ARE THE CHAMPIONS OF THE WORLD!

As the Brazilian team took the field, the players were delighted to see the Maracanã at full capacity—an estimated two hundred thousand people, which remains, even today, the biggest crowd ever to see a soccer game. Before the game started, the team was presented with gold watches carrying the inscription: FOR THE CHAMPIONS OF THE WORLD. And then, just in case anybody missed the point, the governor of Rio de Janeiro state addressed the team, the crowd and the nation:

"You Brazilians, whom I consider victors of the tournament . . . You players who in less than a few hours will be acclaimed by millions of your compatriots . . . You have no equals in the terrestrial hemisphere . . . You who are so superior to every other competitor . . . You whom I already salute as conquerors!"

Amid all of this exaltation, there was only one voice of caution. But it came from a pretty worrying source.

"This isn't an exhibition. It's a match like any other, only harder," Brazil's coach, Flávio Costa, told reporters the day before the game. "I'm afraid that my players will take the field as though they already had the championship shield sewn on their jerseys."

9

All of this raises the question: *Man*, Brazil, what was with all the hype?

Were we being naïve? Stupid?

Or was there something else going on?

One thing I've learned over the years—sometimes the hard way—is that what's happening on the soccer field almost never tells the full story. This is true not just in Brazil, but in countries all over the world. You always have to look outside those white lines—at the players' lives, the teams themselves, and very often, the political situation in the country—to figure out what's really going on.

At the 1950 World Cup, it was especially obvious that sport was only one part of the story. For the first time, but certainly not the last, Brazilian politicians saw the tournament as a golden opportunity to enhance our country's reputation—as well as their own. During that era, Brazil was still seen by many people in Europe and the United States as a tropical backwater, a banana republic, awash in diseases like cholera and dysentery, populated mostly by Indians and illiterate former slaves. If that sounds harsh, or politically incorrect . . . that's because it was. But it was a view that was repeated even by many Brazilian officials, including the mayor of Rio, who declared that the World Cup was a chance to show the world that we were not "savages," and that Brazil could compete with the rich countries of the world—and win.

This was a grossly one-sided way of seeing Brazil, which in reality had been charming outsiders for centuries with its many positive attributes. In fact, even the story of our independence was one of seduction. Unlike most of Latin America, Brazil had been colonized not by the Spanish, but the Portuguese. In 1808, the Portuguese royal family, fleeing Napoleon's invading armies, fled Lisbon and moved the court to Rio de Janeiro—and in so doing, became the first European royals ever to set foot in one of their colonies, much less relocate there. Yet the revealing thing is that, even after Napoleon was defeated and his armies no longer posed a threat, some of the royal family—including the prince regent's son, Pedro I—decided to stay behind.

Why? Well, look—I've been to Lisbon many times, and it's a very cool city. But in Rio, you've got powdery sand, quarter moon–shaped bays, lush, green mountains, and beautiful, diverse, welcoming people. Pedro I could walk out of his palace every morning down a short street lined with king palm trees to take a dip in the Flamengo Bay, all while admiring a view of Sugar Loaf Mountain. So when the rest of the royal family sent him a letter in 1822 demanding he return to Portugal, Pedro I did the logical thing—he told them to go to hell. *"Fico!"* he declared. "I'm staying!" And just like that, with no bloodshed at all, Brazil was born as an independent nation. It was September 7, the day my first soccer team was named after—known still as the day of the "Fico."

It's a lovely story, and one that is hardly an aberration—you never needed to be a monarch to properly enjoy Brazil. Many millions of immigrants from all over the world also came here, became entranced by the people and the possibilities, and decided to stay. But the story of Pedro I also sheds some light on why our government's officials were feeling so nervous in 1950—more than a century had passed since independence, but our politics were still a mess. Since the "Fico," Brazil had lurched from one crisis to another, constantly beset by revolutions and coups and regional uprisings. Just two decades earlier, São Paulo had risen up in a failed revolt against the government in Rio. During World War II, Brazilian soldiers had bravely fought on the side of the Allies—on the side of democracy—only to return home to a dictatorship. As the World Cup began, Brazil was taking baby steps toward progress, but its place in the modern world still seemed very uncertain. "Brazil was a country without glory, fresh out of a dictatorship, in the doldrums of the Dutra government," wrote Pedro Perdigão, in his book about the 1950 World Cup. In other words: Our politicians felt, especially in 1950, like they had something to prove. And they were counting on soccer to help them do so.

Finally, there was one other big issue that was looming over everything in 1950. This was another piece of history, and it was one that was particularly meaningful for the Nascimento family.

We think, based on research that journalists have done over the years, that our ancestors originally came from what is today Nigeria or Angola. The Nascimento name itself was probably adopted from a ranching family in Brazil's northeast. Indeed, our ancestors were among as many as 5.8 million slaves who were brought to Brazil over the years. That's nearly twenty times as many as came to the United States, according to some estimates. At one point, there were probably more slaves in Brazil than free people! Brazil was also one of the world's last countries to abolish the practice, in 1888—more than two decades after the end of the American Civil War.

Slavery was, in other words, a huge part of our country's story. Fernando Henrique Cardoso, a renowned sociologist who became president of Brazil in the 1990s (and my boss, for a few years!), once called it "the root cause of Brazilian inequality." Now, it's true that we never had enforced segregation of the races like America did—in part because there had been a whole lot of, shall we say, intermingling over the years. As a result, anybody trying to determine who was white or black would have had a heck of a headache on their hands. Violence between "blacks" and "whites" was also rare. It was commonly said, especially when I was growing up in the 1950s, that Brazil was a "racial democracy." *Sports Illustrated* once wrote that I lived "happily in one of the few places in the world where color has no effect on a man's life."

But that was only half true: The freed slaves, and their descendants in Brazil, had a tougher life than most. While there was no official discrimination, in practice black Brazilians often had no access to schools, hospitals or any of the other things that could help you move forward in life. I think about the poverty that I grew up in, and that my parents experienced when they were children, and I think our history must have played a role, even if it wasn't always obvious how. Slavery certainly wasn't a distant or abstract idea for our family—Dona Ambrosina, my grandmother who lived with us, was herself the daughter of slaves. Our family was proud of the progress we'd made, and I was— and I am—very proud to be black. But it was also evident, then as now, that the darker your skin in Brazil, the poorer you tended to be.

As a result, even by 1950, Brazil remained a country of mostly poor, sometimes very desperate people who often didn't have enough to eat. This knowledge has always made Brazilian politicians a little bit uneasy. And it probably also helps explain why the hype machine for the World Cup was cranked up to high gear. In the end, officials in Rio weren't just trying to convince the world that progress was coming to Brazil—they were desperately trying to convince their own people!

In later years, we'd feel pretty silly about the way we acted in 1950. But I believe that, when Dondinho said things like "That Cup is ours!" he was probably repeating things he heard on the radio. Those things, in turn, came from the politicians—sometimes on direct orders to the media. All of Brazil got caught up in this propaganda, and it would bleed onto the soccer field in the most unfortunate ways. That was something I'd see throughout my life, again and again and again and again.

10

As our friends and family filed into the house, I had one last question.

"Dad?"

"Yes, Dico?"

"Can I go downtown with you to the celebration?"

I could see my mom, violently shaking her head no, out of the corner of my eye. But Dad just pretended he couldn't see her.

"All right," he said with a smile. "Not for long, but just for a little while."

Delirious with happiness, I floated over to the radio to listen as closely as I could to the action. The massive crowd in the Maracanã was roaring with excitement. The radio announcers were introducing, one by one, the players from the Brazilian team. They were a formidable squad— a mix of skilled players and vivid personalities. There was Zizinho, my favorite player of the Brazilian national team, a man many compared to Leonardo da Vinci because of his artistry on the field. Barbosa, the ace goalie, who had allowed just four goals in our six games. Ademir—the Jaw! And Bigode, a left back who was playing at the time for Flamengo, one of the big clubs in Rio, and got a big cheer as he took the field.

Finally, the radio announcer called out the name of the captain of the 1950 team. He was a feared defender and inspirational leader who seemed immune to the pressure of big games. Perhaps that was because of his past—prior to his playing career, he had been an agent for the Brazilian federal police. He wasn't much of a scorer, even by the standards of defenders—in two hundred ninety-seven games playing for the Brazilian club team Vasco da Gama, he scored exactly zero goals. But the man was a rock on defense, and a soothing presence on the field, perfect for a championship game such as this.

The captain's name? Augusto.

It was the very same Augusto who, some eight years before, had collided with my dad on that field in Minas Gerais.

That's luck for you—one man recovers and goes on to captain Brazil, while another goes back to Baurú, his knee a wreck, to listen to the game on the radio.

If Dad felt jealous that day, he never said so. I suspect he just wanted Brazil to win.

11

The first half of the game was marked by nonstop action, with Brazil constantly on the attack. Our formidable offense, comprised of five forwards, led by the fearsome Jaw, rained shot after shot upon the Uruguayan goal. People who attended the game said that the score could have been 2–0, or even 3–0, in Brazil's favor by the end of the first half. Yet the Uruguayan goalie, Roque Máspoli, somehow managed to stop every single ball that came his way. Some of the saves were pretty lucky, people said. In fact, in coming years, Roque would gain a reputation as a very fortunate guy—twice in his life, he ended up with the winning ticket for the Uruguayan national lottery. So I guess that July 16, 1950, wasn't the only day in Roque's life that the ball bounced his way.

As the second half began, Friaça finally got that first goal past him. As my mom and dad hugged, my friends and I sprinted out of the house and into the neighborhood. Fireworks and rockets were going off everywhere, and my ears buzzed with a delightful hum. Inside the Maracanã, people were throwing confetti and shooting off fireworks as well. The euphoria finally erupted; the national party had begun.

When my friends and I came back inside, the celebration was well under way. My dad and his friends were drinking beer, talking about their games at BAC, not even paying much attention by now to what was being said on the radio.

And then, almost like an afterthought, we heard the announcer for Rádio Nacional blurt out:

"Goal for Uruguay!"

Wait—what?

"Goal for Uruguay!"

The announcer later said he repeated himself precisely because he knew the audience wouldn't believe him the first time.

The room went silent as we listened to his recap of the play.

"A good combination by the Uruguayan attack and it ends with the equalizing goal," the announcer said, sounding suddenly subdued. "Bigode lost out to Ghiggia. He sent in a low cross . . . a lovely cross . . . Schiaffino came in from the left and he scored!"

Brazil 1, Uruguay 1.

Now, there was no reason whatsoever for anybody to panic. That 1950 Cup had a strange, round-robin format, primarily because there were so few teams. As a result, all Brazil had to do was tie Uruguay in that final game, and we would still be crowned champions. Meanwhile, there were only twenty minutes left in the game—our team had allowed an average of less than a goal per game throughout the tournament. Surely our defense wouldn't allow a second goal?

But something strange happened the moment Uruguay knocked that ball into the net. The crowd at the Maracanã felt it, and so did we, even all the way in Baurú. It was as if all the confidence and all the hype suddenly reversed itself, like air rushing out of a room. We'd built ourselves up so high that if we fell, the tumble would be fatal. And suddenly, all of Brazil felt itself staring into the abyss.

I glanced over at Dondinho, who was now wide-eyed, slumped in a chair.

At the Maracanã, a crowd of two hundred thousand people—somehow—went totally quiet.

The silence, Coach Costa later said, "terrified our players."

And little Uruguay, the unwilling underdog, began to smell blood.

12

Soccer has absolutely nothing to do with the size of a country, or the size of the players. Heart, skill and hard work are the only things that matter. My goodness, I should have known that better than anybody.

Somehow, we had forgotten that Uruguay was a country with a soccer tradition at least as rich as ours. Its team was renowned throughout the world for its *"garra charrúa"*—a local term for guts and fighting spirit. They were also known for including players of African descent as early as the 1910s—far earlier than other South American countries, including Brazil. Uruguay already had won two gold medals for soccer at the Olympics, and even had one World Cup championship under its belt—from 1930, the very first Cup, which had been played on Uruguayan soil! That Cup, like the 1950 edition, was also characterized by the absence of several key teams. The world was in the thick of the Great Depression, and many teams from Europe couldn't afford to make the trip. As a result, some people said Uruguay's victory in 1930 had been a fluke. But they should have known better.

When the Uruguayans arrived in Rio for the final, and realized they were being treated as mere patsies in Brazil's coronation, they did exactly what you'd expect from a team with a championship pedigree—they rebelled. The players were absolutely furious, and practiced with unusual intensity. And in their rage, the coaches and the officials accompanying the team saw a golden opportunity.

On the morning of the game, Manuel Caballero, the Uruguayan consul in Rio, picked up twenty copies of that newspaper announcing that Brazil was already the "champions of the world." He took them back to the Hotel Paissandú, where the Uruguayan delegation was staying. When the players sat down for their pregame meal, Caballero dropped the newspapers on the table and declared:

"My condolences; you've all been beaten."

The players exploded in shouting and groans. One of them, Eusebio Tejera, who had a reputation for being a bit emotional, stood up and punched the wall.

"No, no, no! They are not champions!" he screamed. "We'll see who will be the champion!"

According to another account, the Uruguayan team captain, Obdulio Varela, then took the newspapers down to the players' bathroom at the hotel. He scattered them around the room, and the players proceeded to urinate on the pictures of the Brazilian players.

Whatever nerves the Uruguayan players might have had left upon taking the field at the Maracanã later that day, they dissipated when the first half ended scoreless. Brazil's sense of invincibility had been punctured for good. Even when we scored at the start of the second half, that only added to the Uruguayans' siege mentality. Obdulio grabbed the ball from the net and spent a full minute yelling at everyone: the referee, the crowd. He wouldn't let go of the ball. When he finally put it back down on the grass, allowing play to resume, he screamed at his teammates:

"We win here, or they'll kill us!"

Well, that was a bit of hyperbole, but he certainly wasn't the first person in Brazil to exaggerate that day. The rest of the team responded with the urgency Obdulio hoped for, and the equalizing goal soon followed. After that, it was up to Alcides Ghiggia, an outstanding player on the right wing of the field, who, with about ten minutes left to play, found himself almost alone near the Brazilian goal.

13

The call on the radio said it all:

"Ghiggia gives the ball back . . . Julio Perez hits it deep to the right winger . . . Ghiggia bears down on goal . . . and he shoots. It's a goal. Goal for Uruguay! Ghiggia! Uruguay's second goal! Uruguay are 2–1 up . . . Thirty-three minutes gone . . ."

14

Perhaps sensing our imminent defeat, perhaps freaked-out by the silence in our living room, or perhaps just because I was a kid, I went outside to play with my friends before Uruguay scored that second goal. We knocked the ball around halfheartedly, and celebrated a few goals of our own. But we could tell things weren't going well inside.

A short time later, my dad's friends began slowly drifting out of our house, shuffling their feet, anguished looks on their face. At that point, obviously, I knew. I set the ball down on the ground, took a deep breath, and went back inside.

Dondinho was standing with his back toward the room, staring out the window.

"Dad?"

He turned around—with tears rolling down his cheeks.

I was stunned. I had never seen my dad cry before.

"Brazil lost," he croaked, as if barely able to say the words. "Brazil lost."

15

"Never in my life did I see a people as sad as the Brazilians after that defeat," Alcides Ghiggia, who scored the winning goal, recalled years later. He added, showing slightly less empathy: "Only three people in history have managed to silence the Maracanã with a single gesture—the Pope, Frank Sinatra, and me."

When the final whistle blew, thousands of people in the stands began to weep. God knows how many followed suit throughout Brazil. The mood was so grim that, even as the Uruguayans waited for Jules Rimet, the FIFA president and creator of the World Cup, to come out on the field and give them their well-deserved trophy, some of them just wanted to go running into the dressing room. "I cried more than the Brazilians," said Schiaffino, who had scored the first goal, "because I could see how they were suffering."

Outside the Maracanã, angry crowds set fire to stacks of newspapers—including, one assumes, the editions that had prematurely proclaimed Brazil the champion. The stadium didn't burn down, but a statue the mayor had erected of himself outside its doors was pulled to the ground, and the decapitated head tossed into the nearby Maracanã

River. The Brazilian players wandered out of the arena in a daze a few hours later. Many staggered into nearby bars, where some of them spent the next several days. Friaça, who scored Brazil's only goal, was recognized by a group of fans who began shouting the names of the victorious Uruguayan players: "Obdulio!" "Ghiggia!" As Friaça said: "I saw that those shouts were going to follow me for the rest of my life."

Indeed, in ensuing weeks and months, the grief would get only more intense. As loud as the hype had been, the mourning and soul-searching was even louder. It was like the end of a war, with Brazil as the loser, and many dead. The defeat was chalked up not to the short-comings of eleven players, but to the failings of an entire country, proof that Brazil was condemned to eternal backwardness and underdevelopment. Some people began grumbling that Brazil would never win a World Cup, and would never be able to compete at anything with the great countries of the world.

Even some very serious people took this view. Roberto DaMatta, a famous anthropologist, said the loss was maybe the biggest tragedy in Brazil's modern history, because it convinced everyone that we were a nation of losers. Even worse, it came at precisely the time when the country had dared to dream of greatness, in both sport and in terms of global prestige—we had taken a risk, stuck our necks out, and it had gone horribly awry. Years would pass before our national self-esteem recovered. "Every country has its irremediable national catastrophe, something like Hiroshima," wrote Nelson Rodrigues, a Brazilian sports journalist. "Our catastrophe, our Hiroshima, was the defeat by Uruguay in 1950." Another journalist, Roberto Muylaert, would compare the grainy, black-and-white film of Ghiggia's winning goal to footage of the assassination of President John F. Kennedy, saying they both had "the same drama . . . the same movement, rhythm . . . the same precision of an inexorable trajectory."

Some of the players from that 1950 team would go on to great things in their careers at club teams. But, sadly, none of them would ever win a World Cup. Some went to their deathbeds thinking about the one that got away. Zizinho, my favorite player from that team, said he kept his World Cup runners-up medal hidden in a corner of one of his trophy cases, letting it turn black with tarnish. "I don't clean it," he said years later. "In Brazil, being runner-up is garbage. It's better to lose before the final." But even if he tried to forget, other people wouldn't let him. Every July 16, for decades afterward, Zizinho had to take his home phone off the hook. "Otherwise, it rings all day," he grumbled, "with people from all over Brazil, asking why we lost the World Cup."

As bad as that sounds, there was one group of players that got more grief than anyone—the black ones. In his famous book *The Negro in Brazilian Soccer*, the renowned journalist Mário Filho wrote that many Brazilians blamed the defeat on the country's "racial inferiority"—the idea that a black nation with black players was always going to fall short. This was an old and disgusting theory, of course, but it was made worse by the fact—a coincidence—that the Brazilian team's two "blackest" players were both involved in the two Uruguayan goals. Bigode, the defender who was assigned to Schiaffino on the first goal, would be taunted for years afterward as a "coward." He became a recluse, unwilling to socialize with his friends from the 1950 team out of fear someone would mention the game. And Barbosa, the goalie . . . man, that guy had it worst of all.

I would meet Barbosa many times in later years. He lived in Rio, and he continued to play for club teams until 1962, retiring at the advanced age of forty-one after accumulating many other triumphs in his career. But for all his efforts, there was no way for him to escape the finger-pointing, the ridicule, and the anger directed toward him—even decades afterward. Barbosa attempted to visit the Brazilian national team at their training grounds in Teresópolis in 1994, hoping to see them off with an inspiring message prior to the World Cup in the United States—but the team denied him, believing he was "bad luck." Before he passed away in April of 2000, he would often say, to me and many other people: "In this country, the maximum criminal sentence is thirty years. I'm not a criminal, and I already served far more than that."

The hard truth is that Brazil's loss wasn't the fault of Barbosa, or any other player. Zizinho said that all the triumphalist talk in newspapers and elsewhere was "the biggest weapon you can give your adversary." Coach Costa summed it up best of all, attributing the loss to the "atmosphere of 'We already won!' that prevailed among the fans, the press and the management." It was the hype machine that did Brazil in. Everyone who tried to use the game to their advantage, especially the politicians, deserved a share of the blame. They created unrealistic expectations, and the moment it became clear they couldn't be achieved, the Brazilian team was doomed.

"It wasn't the second goal that defeated us," Costa said, "but the first one."

Nevertheless, many people would never accept such excuses. And sadly, the ghosts from the Maracanã still haven't completely left us, even today. Barbosa said the worst day of his life was not July 16, 1950, but a perfectly ordinary afternoon some two decades later, when a woman and her young son spotted him at a store.

"Look at him," the woman said, pointing at Barbosa, speaking loudly enough for him to hear. "That is the man that made all of Brazil cry."

16

Wait—didn't I say that the 1950 World Cup loss was a *good* thing for Brazil?

Bear with me here.

Yes, there were a lot of terrible consequences. For Barbosa, and a great many other people, there was never any silver lining at all. But for the rest of us, that day in Rio was a big learning experience—something that would help forge us as a people, and reverberate in positive ways for decades to come.

Standing around the radio, and suffering together, gave Brazilians a shared experience. For the first time in our history, rich and poor Brazilians alike had something in common, something they could discuss with anybody on the street corner, at the bakery, or at the office, whether they were in Rio, Baurú, São Paulo or deep in the Amazon. We take this sort of thing for granted now; but it was very important back then, in creating a common story of what it meant to be Brazilian. We weren't strangers anymore. And I don't think we ever really were again.

Just as important, Brazilians also lost a bit of that blinking innocence, that youngness—you could call it gullibility, even—that had been so evident on that July afternoon, and in the months prior. It wouldn't disappear, by any means. But afterward we were all just a little more mature, and a little less likely to accept whatever politicians, or the media, were trying to tell us. This would have big consequences, on our politics and on our culture, in years to come.

Finally: For a generation of aspiring soccer players like me, July 16, 1950, was motivating in ways that I couldn't possibly exaggerate. As I watched my dad cry, and my mom trying to comfort him, I slipped into my parents' room. They had a picture of Jesus on the wall. I burst into tears as I addressed Him.

"Why did this happen?" I sobbed. "Why did it happen to us? Why, Jesus, why are we being punished?"

There was no answer, of course. But as my despair subsided, it was replaced by something else—something deeper, and more mellow. I dried my tears, walked into the living room, and put my hand on my dad's arm.

As for what I said next—honestly, I don't know where it came from. Maybe it was just one of those things a nine-year-old boy says to make a parent feel better. But it certainly was interesting, given everything that would happen later.

"It's OK, Dad," I told him. "One day, I promise, I'll win the World Cup for you."

SWEDEN, 1958

1

Our bus chugged up the mountain, belching black smoke and straining with every shift of the gears. At one point, we seemed to roll backward, and I began praying to God to please, please let us survive this trip. I pressed my face to the window, hoping to see a lush field of grass or some other soft, benevolent thing that might cushion our fall if we tipped over. No such luck—only a rocky outcropping, covered with a thick tangle of emerald jungle. Beyond that, barely visible, the distant skyscrapers and factories of São Paulo, which we were now leaving behind, headed for the Atlantic coast.

I took a deep breath. This day was already terrifying enough, even without the risk of a fiery death. I was on my way to audition for the Santos Football Club, a relatively small but successful team in a port city by the same name. I had spent the last few years playing for the youth team associated with the BAC, Dondinho's club in Baurú. The youth coach, Waldemar de Brito, was an accomplished soccer virtuoso who had played on Brazil's 1934 World Cup team. Waldemar was certain that I possessed a special talent. So he had arranged for my tryout with people he knew at Santos. Dondinho and I had taken the train from Baurú to São Paulo earlier that morning, where we met up with Waldemar and had lunch. Now the three of us were on the bus headed for Santos.

Leaving Baurú had been heart wrenching. First, I had to say goodbye to all my friends from the neighborhood—the boys I'd been playing soccer with for years. And then, the night before my departure, the whole family gathered one last time to see me off. My grandmother, Dona Ambrosina, cried inconsolably. Everybody else held things together pretty well though, including—somewhat surprisingly—my mom. She still had deep misgivings about soccer, but Waldemar had spent long hours in our house, working to assure her that my skills were truly extraordinary, a gift from God, just like Dondinho had always said. Waldemar even sobbed as he pleaded with her, saying it would be a sin to keep a player like me penned up in Baurú. And in any case, if it didn't work out after a month of tryouts, he said I could come back home.

I guess his argument was convincing enough. Right before I left, Mom presented me with two pairs of long pants she had sewn for me, special for the trip. They were the first long pants I'd ever owned—up until that point in my life, as I ran around Baurú, I'd needed only to wear shorts.

"I know you'll make us proud, Dico," she said. "If you remember everything we taught you, and you stay out of trouble, there'll be nothing to worry about."

I had my doubts. And first, there was this little matter of the mountain.

Along we crawled, making agonizing hairpin turns and going over bridges that seemed to be floating on top of the clouds. It seemed unnatural, almost against God's will, for us to be driving so high in the air. I worried that He might change his mind, and send us flying back down the mountain backward—all the way back to Baurú.

The whole time, probably seeing how nervous I was, Waldemar was whispering advice into my ear, while Dad slept in the seat behind us.

"Don't talk to the press—they'll just try to make you look foolish."

"Beware of cigarettes. They'll make you run more slowly."

"Women: They're trouble!"

Unfortunately, I didn't hear half of what Waldemar was saying, even though I certainly could have used the advice. I was already thinking too much about our destination—and one thing in particular, which excited me more than anything.

Before I knew it, we were pulling into the city of Santos, bound for the bus station. We passed the railway yards, the red-roofed mansions on the hills, and the narrow maze of streets downtown. Finally, down one of the city's many long, straight boulevards, I spotted the thing I had been most eager to see. It shimmered there in the distance, blue and impossibly large—much larger than I had imagined. I was so excited that I think I screamed, waking up the other passengers on the bus.

"Calm down, boy!" Waldemar hissed, laughing with surprise. "We'll take you there soon enough!"

I was fifteen years old, just a boy from Baurú seeing the ocean for the first time.

Barely two years later, I would be carried around the field on the shoulders of my teammates, having just helped Brazil win our first World Cup title.

2

I t amazes me, even now, to think how quickly everything changed.

Those two years were like being on a rocket ship—thrilling but slightly out of control, always headed higher but with a destination that was totally uncertain. At various points, there was little I could do but close my eyes and enjoy the ride.

But this to me is not a story about fame, or glory. It's not even really about sport, per se. It's a story about realizing that I was *really* good at something.

I believe that every single person has a talent, a gift. Some people are even blessed with more than one. It could be art; it could be music. It could be mathematics or curing disease. The important thing is to discover one's talent, work hard to perfect it, and then—hopefully—be lucky enough to use that talent and be properly recognized for it. Being able to do all those things in a relatively short time, from 1956 to 1958, was the greatest and most gratifying adventure of my life.

I know that my experience was not typical in many ways. But I have friends who are doctors, business executives, schoolteachers and nurses, and they speak of their self-discovery using many of the same terms that I do. The pleasure of excelling, of really being the best, is something that everyone should be able to feel. There's nothing quite like it—and it doesn't matter if there are sixty thousand people watching, or nobody at all. If you can find that thing that you're good at, that makes you happy, it will fulfill you for as long as you walk this earth. For me, as for countless millions of boys and girls around the world, that thing was soccer.

3

When I walked into the Santos stadium on that first day, it seemed like anything *but* the start of something big. In fact, I felt like I was about three feet tall.

We arrived on a Sunday, and there was a game in progress—Santos versus Comercial, a game for the São Paulo state championship, the main league my new team played in. Waldemar got the three of us some seats, and I watched in awe. I'd never seen a game of this caliber before, not even as a spectator—and of course there was no television in those days either. The action moved at a velocity that seemed unreal. I had even heard of several of the players, including Jair da Rosa Pinto, who had been on that ill-fated 1950 Brazilian national team at the Maracanã. I kept blinking my eyes, again and again, unable to fathom that I might soon be playing alongside these guys.

The game ended, and Waldemar escorted Dondinho and me underneath the stands to the locker room. After I was introduced to the coach—Luis Alonso, known as Lula—the first player I met was Válter Vasconcelos, a great attacking midfielder who over the course of his career scored more than one hundred goals for Santos. He wore the number ten shirt—traditionally worn by the team's field general, the player who distributes the ball around the field, a bit like the quarterback in American football.

Vasconcelos put his arm around my neck and flashed a grin at my dad.

"Don't worry," he said in a low rumble. "We'll take care of the boy!"

I smiled, relief washing over me. But that feeling didn't last long. Before I fully realized what was happening, Dondinho was giving me a hug good-bye.

"Everything will be OK," he said quietly. "You'll be a big success."

And then, just like that, Dondinho walked out of the locker room with Waldemar, headed back to Baurú, and the only life I had ever known.

I stood there, watching the door for a minute, sort of expecting them to come walking back through at any moment. It was as if, in a single instant, my childhood had ended. And in a way, it had.

I have to admit, those first few nights after Dondinho left were desperately lonely. I was sleeping in the stadium itself, in a dorm room underneath the bleachers where Santos had put bunk beds for the single players. The other guys were very kind, and did their best to make me comfortable. But it didn't feel much like home—the room was horribly dark, and there were no pictures, no relatives, no homemade rice and beans. I spent my nights thinking of my parents, my brother and sister, and my friends from the old Sete de Setembro team.

Early one morning, I tried to run away back to Baurú. I made it as far as the stadium's front door, but one of the team officials, a nice guy named Sabuzinho, stopped me. He said that because I was a minor, I needed written permission to leave the building. I told him not to worry, that I'd just bring a note back to him later. God knows what I was thinking—I had no money, no means of getting anywhere. Luckily, Sabuzinho saw through my ploy—well, let's be honest, he didn't have to be a genius to see what I was doing—and he sent me back to my room, where I stayed.

There was no one moment when things started to turn around for me. There was no epiphany or great triumph. Instead, I just kept training, kept doing my drills, kept focusing on soccer. Some mornings I'd wake up, and my head felt like it was filled with fog, making it physically hard to move. But I'd fight my way out of my bunk, and get myself to the practice field. And soon enough, once we started dribbling and passing and shooting, the fog would disappear. Every single time.

Santos said I was still too small—literally too tiny, since I weighed only about a hundred and twenty pounds—to play any games with the first team. At first the older players had me fetch them coffee, cigarettes and sodas—more errand boy than teammate. But they did have me training with the big boys. And it didn't take long for me to realize that I was indeed capable of keeping pace with the top players.

In one practice, Coach Lula assigned a player named Formiga ("Ant") to cover me—a really good defender who had even played a few games for the Brazilian national team. I was able to dribble past him twice, and send a bunch of balls into the goal.

"You're looking good, kid," Lula said. "Keep working. And eat! My God, you've got to get bigger!"

This wasn't hard advice to follow. With good sources of protein like chicken and beef regularly available to me for the first time in my life, I ate everything in sight, while continuing to exercise constantly. Santos had a gym, and I began learning karate, which was very useful in learning how to jump properly—and, just as important in soccer, how to fall. My body started filling out with muscle. My legs got so big that, before long, my thighs had the same circumference as my waist. In the meantime, I did all the basic drills I'd performed since I was a kid, at Dondinho's instruction. I spent hours on the field, kicking the ball around long after the other players had departed.

I realized that, even if I was far away from home, I was doing what I loved.

I was happy.

And although I didn't realize it yet, I was on my way up.

4

ondinho always told me that to succeed in soccer, talent was important—but it wasn't sufficient. His story certainly proved that. Indeed, he always said that you had to have luck, too. Those words were ringing in my ears in mid-1956 as I was trying to figure out how to get on the field for Santos.

My first games were for Santos' youth team. I scored quite a few goals, enough to convince the club to declare my tryout a success and sign me to a real contract—even if it wasn't particularly legal, given that I was still only a minor. After a few more junior matches, my shot at the big-time finally came. Well, sort of. The main Santos team had a practice match—a "friendly," as they're called—in the nearby city of Cubatão. Several of the regular players weren't able to go, so I donned a first-team jersey for the first time and took the field. We won 6–1, and I scored four goals.

After that, the other players started to treat me a bit differently. In addition, the media in Santos began paying attention, writing stories about the kid from the interior who could do amazing things with the ball. Word spread, and we started getting crowds of ten thousand people or more for Santos' practice sessions—twice the usual number.

On September 7, 1956—Brazil's independence day, the day for which my neighborhood team had been named—I got into a first-team game for Santos that officially counted, against Corinthians. This wasn't the well-known Corinthians team, but a smaller team with the same name from Santo André, one of the industrial suburbs of São Paulo. Almost as soon as I got on the field, one of Santos' best players, Pepe, took a shot on goal. The goalie knocked the ball out, and I managed to score on the rebound—my first official goal as a professional player, the first of more than 1,280 goals that I would score in my career. I was thrilled, and I ran around the field punching the air with delight. When the game was over, the Corinthians' crowd stood and applauded us. The players were also very kind, and came over to congratulate me.

It was a good debut. The Santos media began openly calling for the team to get me into games more regularly. People around town started to recognize me too, and ask me when I'd start playing more often.

I was prepared to wait. I had started off at Santos as an *armador*, a supporting midfielder. But I was now being used mostly as an attacking midfielder—the number ten spot. The issue with this was that Santos already had two really good attacking midfielders on the field—Del Vecchio and Vasconcelos, the guy who had put his arm around me and welcomed me so warmly on my first day with the club.

Given my family's history, I just hate that things happened the way they did. One afternoon when Santos was playing São Paulo in a championship game at home, Vasconcelos had a terrible collision with an opposing player. As he writhed about on the field, all of us realized it was serious—and it was. Vasconcelos' leg was broken.

His injury turned out to be the opening that put me on the field for good. When the season started up again in early 1957, and Vasconcelos still hadn't fully recovered, I took his place. I would never really give it up again.

Vasconcelos was the consummate gentleman when, years later, reporters asked him how the whole thing went down.

"The Santos number ten shirt was unquestionably mine," he said, "until the arrival of a little black boy with sticks for legs, who entered history as Pelé."

5

There have been lots of crazy theories over the years about the origin of the nickname "Pelé." One is that it came from the Gaelic word for soccer—which is neat, but doesn't explain why a boy from Baurú would be called that. Pelé also means "wonder" or "marvel" in Hebrew—but that hypothesis falls short for the same reason. One of the more elaborate theories is that a group of Turkish merchants in Baurú once saw my friends and me playing, and I accidentally touched the ball with my hands. So they said "Pé"—which is Portuguese for "foot"—and "le," which may or may not mean "stupid" in Turkish. Actually, that theory makes no sense at all, but believe it or not it has been mentioned in previous books about me, so I'm only repeating it here to demonstrate the extent of the confusion during all these years!

So what's the truth?

The truth is actually a little bit disappointing: Nobody knows for certain where "Pelé" came from. That's because the name is utter gibberish—it means absolutely nothing in Portuguese. But there *is* one theory, which comes from my uncle Jorge, that seems much more credible than the others, and it has to do with those pickup soccer games we used to play back in Baurú.

As I've mentioned, I used to play goalie a lot, because otherwise, if I was on offense the whole game, our team would start winning big and the kids from the opposing team would lose interest. Well, during those very early years, the goalie on Dondinho's semiprofessional team was a guy nicknamed "Bilé." So when I played in goal, the other kids in the neighborhood would say—"Hey, he thinks he's Bilé!" "Look, Bilé saved another shot!" Since we were so young, the name got twisted around, and the vowels and consonants became a little mangled. "Bilé" evolved into "Pelé." And before long, that was the nickname that followed me around on the soccer field.

Growing up, I *hated* that damn nickname. After all, it was a garbage word that meant nothing. Plus, I was really proud of the name Edson, believing it was an honor to be named after such an important inventor. Things even got to the point where I'd fight other kids who called me "Pelé." If they insisted on a nickname, I could definitely tolerate "Dico," and there was a period where my nickname on the field was "Gasolina"—because I was fast, I guess. But no matter what I did, I couldn't rid myself of "Pelé."

When I got to Santos, though, something changed. And I began to think of the Pelé nickname in a whole new way.

This is a tough one to explain. But here goes: As my career began to really take off, I started thinking of "Pelé" almost as a separate identity. Edson was the poor kid from Baurú, the son of Dondinho and Dona Celeste, the boy who desperately missed his family back home. Pelé was the rising star who, while still a teenager, would become a sporting icon and perhaps the world's most famous athlete. Edson could be reserved and shy. But Pelé could play the crowd and flash his smile for the cameras. They were the same person, but represented two different realities—one familiar to me, and one that was new, constantly changing, and sometimes a little scary.

Does that sound crazy? Maybe so. But remember that I was barely sixteen when I became a regular for Santos. I was an immediate sensation—I was the top goal scorer in the São Paulo state league that very first year. This took place during an era, the late 1950s, when radio and other mass media were just starting to take off in Brazil. For the first time, there was a kind of popular culture, and I was abruptly thrust into the center of it. Overnight, I was surrounded by journalists and fans and people who said they wanted to be my friend. Our society is accustomed to celebrity now, and even cynical about it, but at the time nobody else had really been through any of this before. For a boy like me, it was all pretty overwhelming. Not on the field—there, I was always in control—but off of it. So, the persona I adopted was a kind of defense mechanism, a little barrier between me and the world. It allowed me to keep my feet on the ground as a person. Having Pelé around helped keep Edson sane.

Over the years, I've raised eyebrows by sometimes referring to Pelé in the third person. "Pelé scored two goals today, but he felt . . ." "Pelé is very happy to be here in Berlin." This was often out of necessity. There were aspects of being Pelé that were almost impossible to understand, even—or especially—for me. Being the object of so much love has been a true honor—I've been humbled by the good wishes I've received from all over the world. One writer, Norman Cutler, once wrote: "In the course of half an hour, he is showered with more hero-worship than a normal player receives during his whole career." I don't treat this lightly. God blessed me with an extraordinary talent, and I've always felt that it was my solemn obligation to Him to use that talent to make as many people happy as I could. That's one reason why, to this day, I never turn down anyone who wants an autograph or a photo with me.

I've seen amazing things over the years—things that go beyond the normal interaction between an athlete and a fan. I've seen grown men burst into tears upon seeing me; I've had literally all of my clothes ripped off by souvenir-seeking fans after big games; I've been mobbed by screaming, sobbing women; supposedly, they once even declared a truce in a civil war in Africa so that I could play a game there.

When I lived in New York City in the 1970s, I would often visit children's hospitals. Kids who hadn't left their beds in months would rise to their feet, seemingly cured, when I entered the room. Their eyes would light up, and they'd say: "I'm going to be a famous soccer player! I'm going to score lots of goals, just like you, Pelé!"

Some of these kids had terminal cancer. My goodness, sometimes they'd be missing a leg. But I'd glance over at the parents, and they'd have this light in their eyes, like they believed it, too. So I'd look back at the child, nod and say, with as much conviction as I could muster:

"That's right, son, you're going to get out of here and be a great soccer player, just like me."

Being part of this was a tremendous privilege, some of the richest and most fulfilling experiences I ever had. Lord, I cry now just thinking about it. But these kids weren't excited about meeting some Brazilian guy named Edson. They were summoning what little strength they had left to see Pelé, the soccer legend, the icon. It was almost too much for one person to handle. Living up to those huge expectations—being Pelé—would, over the years, be just as challenging as anything I ever did on the field.

6

ate one afternoon, I went downstairs to the manager's office at the
Santos stadium, so I could make my weekly phone call back home
to Baurú.

Dondinho sounded out of breath as he picked up the receiver.

"Dico," he said, "I think you've been called up to the national team!"

I began shouting with excitement, and even did a little celebratory
dance, right there in the office. This meant that I would be on the team
in time to compete for the 1958 World Cup, at the age of only seventeen!

"Wait—wait just a moment, son. Take it easy," Dondinho said. "I
said I *think* you've been called up."

"You . . . I . . . *What?*"

I felt like my heart was going to explode as Dondinho explained to
me what had happened. He'd been sitting around the house, listening
to the radio, when the announcer began reading out the names of players who had been called up to the national team. But Dondinho said he
couldn't tell if the announcer had said "Pelé" or "Telê"—who was a
player for Fluminense, one of the clubs in Rio.

"Maybe you should go ask the managers," Dondinho suggested. "Then you can call me back."

I slammed down the phone and went sprinting around the club offices underneath the stadium, trying to find somebody—anybody—who could clarify things for me. The first couple of people I saw just shrugged and said they'd heard nothing. Finally, I tracked down Modesto Roma, who was the Santos club chairman at the time.

When I told him about the confusion, he laughed and laughed.

"Oh, he definitely said 'Pelé,'" Roma said. "I received a phone call a few hours ago. Congratulations, kiddo, you've made the national team."

Like I said: that *damn* nickname!

7

was honored and excited to get the call-up, but I also knew exactly what awaited us—a big mess.

Eight years had passed since the disaster at the Maracanã, but Brazil still hadn't moved on—no, not in the slightest. Our team had qualified for the 1954 World Cup, which was played in Switzerland— another country that hadn't fought in World War II, and was therefore in good shape to host the event. The 1954 Cup was notable for a number of reasons—it was the first tournament to be broadcast on television, and the Germans were allowed to compete again. But Brazil was sent home after getting only as far as the quarterfinals, when our team was destroyed 4–2 by a very skilled team from Hungary—the Marvelous Magyars, they were called. The Hungarians, in turn, lost to the West Germans in the championship game.

There was no hysteria this time—in fact, there was little reaction at all, just a kind of big, nationwide shrug. The time difference with Europe meant that many of the games took place very late at night in Brazil. Only a small elite of Brazilians had televisions, and the quality of the radio broadcasts coming from Switzerland also wasn't very good, some said. But the main reason for the apathy was, clearly, that Brazilians still felt burned by 1950. The trauma was still so fresh that people had trouble getting emotionally attached to the 1954 team. And maybe it was just as well.

Following the 1954 tournament, while playing in World Cup qualifying matches against other teams in South America, Brazil had done nothing to shed its growing reputation as a team that played loosely and brilliantly against inferior opponents, but choked against the big guys. In 1957, the Brazilian team beat Ecuador 7–1 and Colombia 9–0, while getting walloped 3–0 by the Argentines and—most agonizing of all—dropping a 3–2 decision to our old nemesis, Uruguay. Needing one last win against Peru to qualify for the 1958 World Cup, Brazil got it by the slimmest of margins—an aggregate 2–1. Meanwhile, the team itself was in organizational disarray, calling up a bewildering and ever-shifting roster of players, and constantly shifting its leadership, with seven different coaches in the previous three years. Four months before the tournament was to start in Sweden, the coaching spot was still vacant.

The team's authorities asked us to report to Rio on April 7. Apart from that, we didn't really know what to expect—and, man, were we in for a surprise! Upon arrival, instead of heading for a practice field to start kicking a ball around, we were sent directly to the Santa Casa de Misericordia, a local hospital.

There, I and the other thirty-two players were submitted to an impressive array of examinations from neurologists, radiologists, dentists, cardiologists and more. We were poked, prodded, massaged, X-rayed and interviewed. The goal? To begin the process of weeding out eleven players. Only twenty-two of us would be making the trip to Sweden.

The theory behind all this: Nobody said so out loud, but these tests were a direct result of the perceived lessons from 1950. That is, if Brazil's chronic poverty and underdevelopment had somehow caused us to lose to Uruguay, then our team was now going to use every scientific tool available to get rid of the players who showed symptoms of these maladies. This was easier said than done. Here, it is worth briefly exploring once again just what a sickly country Brazil still was in the mid-1950s. In some rural areas, half of Brazilian babies died before their first birthday. One out of three Brazilians hosted hookworms. The average life span was just forty-six years, compared to almost seventy in the United States. And while all thirty-three of us there in Rio appeared to be healthy athletes in the prime of our lives, the doctors were determined to discover if any of these pestilences and diseases were lurking right beneath the surface.

To fit the doctors' vision of an ideal athlete, several players had teeth pulled, right then and there. Others were given a quick tonsillectomy. Still others were eventually sent home because their physical makeup wasn't quite right.

Two of the players, above all, merited special scrutiny.

One of them was Manuel Francisco dos Santos, who played on the right wing for the Botafogo club and was better known by his nickname: "Garrincha," or "little bird." Garrincha was, at first glance, the poster child for precisely the kind of defects and illnesses the Brazilian doctors were screening for. His spine was deformed, and his left leg was two and a half inches shorter than his right, which was itself bent grotesquely inward. Garrincha probably wouldn't even have been invited to the team at all if another winger, Julinho, who was playing for a club in Italy, hadn't declined a spot, saying it should go to someone who was still playing in Brazil. Doctors from all over the hospital came to marvel at Garrincha's legs, which were also covered with scars from collisions and kicks that he had absorbed from opponents. Garrincha scored poorly on his mental aptitude test; on the line where he was supposed to fill in his profession, he wrote *"atreta,"* or "athrete." Yet, truth be told, if spelling had been the main criterion, Brazil might not have sent a single player to Sweden in 1958! And the doctors, after considerable scrutiny, concluded his legs, while absolutely horrid to look at, seemed to work fine, more or less. Garrincha was cleared to join the squad.

The second player who was put under the microscope? As you might have guessed, that was me. I scored pretty well on the physical exam and motor skills, but came up short on the behavioral tests that could supposedly measure our mental toughness. These were considered particularly crucial, given the supposed lack of mettle that caused Brazil to lose in 1950. And nobody was in the mood to make any allowances for the fact that, at seventeen, I would be one of the youngest players ever to participate in a World Cup.

The verdict from João Carvalhães, a sociologist who was running the tests, left no room for doubt: "Pelé is obviously infantile," Carvalhães wrote. "He lacks the necessary fighting spirit. He's too young to feel aggression and react with adequate force. What's more, he doesn't have the necessary sense of responsibility to team spirit."

"I don't advise that we take him" to Sweden, Carvalhães concluded.

Luckily, the man who was ultimately chosen as coach of the 1958 team, Vicente Feola, was a man of instinct. After fully reading Carvalhães' report, he replied:

"You may be right. The thing is, you don't know a thing about soccer! If Pelé is healthy, he'll play."

8

Our practices were rigorous and spirited. Our team gelled well, and seemed relatively unburdened by the ghosts of World Cups past. Three days before we departed for Europe, there was just one more hurdle to clear: a final warm-up game against Corinthians, one of Brazil's biggest and most popular club teams, at Pacaembu Stadium in São Paulo.

We should have never, ever played that game.

To this day, I have no idea why the team scheduled it. We had already played warm-up matches against other national teams, including Bulgaria and Paraguay, so we were ready for competition. Playing a local club with a huge fan base like Corinthians produced an odd, predictable and completely undesirable effect: We would be jeered on Brazilian soil before a crowd that was almost entirely against us. Making matters worse, the Corinthians team and their fans were angry over a perceived insult: Their most beloved player, Luizinho, had been left off of the national team.

As we took the field at Pacaembu, boos rained down on the Brazilian team. They only increased in volume as we began scoring goals.

When we were up 3–1, and many players were already thinking about what on earth we'd need to wear to Sweden, I received a pass in our opponent's midfield and began heading for the penalty area. I never even saw Ari Clemente, a Corinthians defender, as he slid toward me.

I felt like someone had stuck a flaming needle deep inside my right knee. I rolled around on the ground, screaming, as the team trainers sprinted toward me.

"Can you get up, son?"

I was overcome with pain—and horror. I thought instantly of my father. It was the same knee that he had ruined in his first big game. Was this to be my destiny too?

"I'm fine, I'm fine," I said, struggling to reassure myself, mostly.

But as I tried to get back on my feet, and put some pressure on the knee, it immediately buckled. The trainers exchanged knowing glances and carried me off the field, back to the dressing room. I was sobbing like a child.

In all the years that followed, and all the big games I played in, I can't recall any moments more unnerving than those initial minutes as I sat in the dark training room at Pacaembu, drying my eyes, with my knee up on a metal table. The medical staff—Dr. Hilton Gosling, the team doctor, and Mário Américo, our beloved physical therapist—put some ice on my knee and talked to each other in hushed tones.

"Don't worry one bit," Mário said. "I'm going to make sure you're just fine."

Kind words, but nobody really knew what would happen. After all, we were still in Brazil, and there were eleven healthy players—including Luizinho—who were more than ready to take my place. It would have been a simple, obvious decision to leave me behind—and I later learned just how close they came to making it. The Brazilian team authorities sounded out a player named Almir, who played for Vasco da Gama, as a replacement for me.

In the end, Dr. Gosling told the coaches that my knee was in fact in pretty bad shape. I would miss up to a month, he said, meaning all the remaining warm-up games we had scheduled in Europe, and probably the first few matches of the World Cup as well. But Dr. Gosling told them I was young and in very good health; and I might, just might, recover more quickly than he anticipated.

The coaches had a long, detailed discussion—and decided that the risk of taking me to Europe was worth the potential payoff. If I had been in charge, I don't know that I would have made the same decision. But for the grace of God, and the faith of the doctors and the coaches, my life could have been quite different.

9

For a few years back in Baurú, I had dreamed of being a pilot. There was a small airstrip in town, and I'd spend long afternoons there sitting by the side of the runway watching planes and gliders take off and land, sometimes skipping school to see the pilots in their leather jackets and aviator glasses. It all looked impossibly glamorous, a passport to a new and more exciting life.

One day, we heard someone shout that a pilot had crashed his glider. This seemed like the most dramatic thing that had ever happened in Baurú. My friends and I ran first to the scene of the accident, where we closely examined the smoldering aircraft. Then we went over to the hospital, and we peered in through a dirty window. Sure enough, there was the dead pilot, lying there on the autopsy table. I was fascinated—I'd never seen a corpse before—but then the doctor tried to move the poor man's arm. This required some effort, as the body must have already been stiff, and as he yanked at it, a stream of blood spilled out onto the floor. My friends and I screamed in horror, and ran home as fast as we could. I had nightmares about it for months, if not years.

Well, as you might imagine, that experience put me off flying for a while. So when I boarded a Panair DC-7 bound for Europe on May 24, 1958, it was the first time I had ever been on an airplane. I ambled slowly up the stairs, my right knee wrapped in a giant bandage, nervous about the trip and—above all—the possibility I might not get to play at all because of my injury. Would I be sent back to Brazil as soon as we arrived in Europe? My stomach was churning.

Once we got under way, though, things lightened up quickly. The team dentist, Dr. Mário Trigo, was a jokester who kept things lively by organizing a kind of quiz game in which he asked us questions and we provided all kinds of goofy answers. When we stopped to refuel in Recife, a city on Brazil's northeastern coast, there were thousands of people at the airport, chanting and cheering, wishing us good luck. This helped remove some of the sour taste from the Corinthians game—and reminded us that we had an entire country on our side.

We also began to forge the personal bonds and friendships that make any team—especially a national team—such a fulfilling experience. Nothing brings people together quite like the honor of representing one's country. And, this being Brazil, one important form of bonding was to assign everybody stupid nicknames, even if they had two or three of them already. Gylmar was "Giraffe," because of his long neck. De Sordi was "Head," because his was huge. Dino Sani was "Knee"—because he was bald, and without hair his head looked like a knee. A few nicknames were so vulgar as to be completely unpublishable. Didi was "Black Heron," and Mazzola was "Stony Face." For reasons of obvious physical irony, everybody thought it would be hilarious to call me "Alemão"—"The German."

Our first port of call in Europe was Lisbon, where we refueled. Then it was on to Italy, where the team had scheduled another two warm-up matches against Italian clubs, Fiorentina of Florence and Internazionale of Milan, both of which I missed because of my knee. Before the games, the team took a bus tour of Rome. We were quite the spectacle—a bunch of country boys from Brazil, yelling and laughing like crazy as we toured the cradle of Western civilization. We saw the Colosseum, the Fountain of Trevi, the Via Veneto, and all the other usual sights. In truth, it was all kind of lost on us—we began chanting "Lunch! Lunch! Lunch!" before the tour was even over. Finally, our coaches gave up and obliged us with a visit to a big Italian restaurant, where we downed giant plates of pasta. This, we understood.

We didn't know much about the world. But then again, the world didn't know much about us, either. When we finally arrived at our hotel in Sweden a few days later, we saw that our hosts had hung flags on poles for each of the countries competing in the World Cup. The Soviet Union, England, Wales . . . they were all there, in good shape. But the flag for Brazil was almost completely wrong. Oh, it was blue, green and yellow, more or less. But instead of a globe in the middle there was a square, and it was horribly out of position.

I was standing there outside the hotel with some of the team's older players: Nilton Santos, Zagallo, Gylmar, and a few others. One of them pointed at the flag, and we all just stood there for a moment in stunned silence. Then somebody started to chuckle, and soon we were all laughing. Finally, Gylmar, the goalie, said:

"Well, damn. I guess we'd better ask them to change the flag."

Gylmar took it upon himself to do so. A short while later, our Swedish hosts graciously put up a new flag that was correct in every way. It was an innocent mistake, but the lesson wasn't lost on any of us: We weren't the only ones who still had some learning to do.

10

t's pretty amazing, in today's world of Facebook and Google and You-Tube and CNN, to remember how little *anyone* knew about other countries back then. Even in 1958, a TV was still a luxury item, available to only a select few in Europe, much less Brazil. So, in Sweden, as on all the other countless trips abroad I'd make in coming years, we were more than soccer players—we were ambassadors. For most people, whether they were watching us from the stands or meeting us on the street, we were the first contact with Brazil they'd ever had. Millions upon millions of people around the world first became acquainted with our country because of soccer in those years. This was an awesome responsibility. It was also great fun.

I was mostly focused on getting my knee healed. But there was only so much time I could spend with an ice pack on my leg, and we had six whole days in Sweden before the real games started. So I joined the other, older players on walks around town. We fell in love with this strange new world pretty quickly.

Of course, the Brazil team management had radically different ideas about what we were supposed to be doing with our time. They were determined to keep us as focused as possible. They may have also wanted to stamp out a bit of the "Brazilianness" that supposedly cost us so dear in 1950. Among the long list of rules and regulations imposed upon us, we were explicitly forbidden from bringing tambourines, noisemakers or drums along with us on the plane. "It was the Brazilian national team that was traveling to Sweden, not a samba school," wrote the journalist Ruy Castro in his book *Estrela Solitária*. We were also prohibited from talking to the press outside of set times, or bringing newspapers or magazines into the training area. The team opened all of our mail from our families, screening it for any news that might upset us before passing it along. Once a week, we were allowed to talk to our families by phone—for three minutes, tops.

It was all pretty restrictive. But there were *other* elements of the Swedish scene that the team, for all its efforts, couldn't do much about. Oh, they tried! For example, Dr. Gosling asked the hotel where we were staying, near the city of Hindas, to temporarily switch out all twenty-eight of its female employees for twenty-eight male ones. Fair enough; the hotel complied. But the players quickly discovered a much more dangerous distraction—a nearby island in one of the Swedish lakes that doubled as a nudist colony, and happened to be (barely) visible from the windows of our hotel. Dr. Gosling asked the Swedish authorities if the people on the island wouldn't mind covering themselves up while the Brazilian team was in town. That request was politely denied. Some of the players on the team somehow acquired binoculars; and we went from there.

Once we established first contact, there was no way to keep the Swedish girls away. This was only 1958, but in retrospect it's clear that the sixties came to Sweden a few years early. The women there were beautiful and tremendously forward, in ways that we'd never seen before in Brazil. To our utter shock, the most popular players on our team were not the tall, handsome ones, but the three black players—Didi, Moacir, and myself. The girls would come running up to us for pictures, or an autograph, or just to chat. We didn't know any Swedish, they didn't know any Portuguese, and the three of us players only had about six words of English among us. But the girls didn't seem to care one bit. I imagine many of them had never seen a black person at all before. Some just wanted to rub their hands on our arms and faces. This, of course, prompted uproarious laughter and teasing from the rest of the team.

"Tell them it doesn't come off, Pelé! You can go out in the rain without worrying!"

I know such comments might seem offensive in today's world, but it really was all in the innocent spirit of discovery back then. The girls did seem genuinely surprised when our blackness didn't just rub off! I even ended up having a little fling with a gorgeous Swedish girl named Ilena, who was also seventeen. Again, we couldn't communicate much, but she had this great laugh, and we'd go walking around town, hand in hand, pointing at things and smiling until my face hurt. We were thrilled to have met each other and to have been swept up in this big, important, exciting global event. I remember Ilena cried when I left town, which made me feel sad but also thrillingly like an adult, to have a person in the world who would miss me in that kind of way.

In the end, the players figured out a way around the ban on communications—sort of. A group of us went out shopping one day. The stores back in Brazil didn't have many imports back then—Brazil was a closed economy, so anything from abroad was very expensive. We saw all kinds of things that were a real revelation for us, including one relatively new invention: battery-powered radios. That afternoon, I was with Garrincha, the player with the bent legs, and Nilton Santos, who was Garrincha's teammate at Botafogo. We were testing the radios, turning them on to see if the speakers worked, when Garrincha got this horrible look on his face, like he'd just smelled a corpse.

"I'm not buying that radio, no way!"

Nilton turned around, surprised. "Why not, Garrincha?"

"I don't understand a damn thing it says!"

It took us a minute, but we figured it out. The voice coming through on the little radio was, obviously, speaking in Swedish.

"Oh, come on, Garrincha!" Nilton roared, gasping for air because he was laughing so hard. "It'll speak Portuguese when you're back in Brazil!"

Garrincha shook his head, still looking confused. "No way, man."

I was laughing too, but it was the kind of mistake I could have easily made myself. As I said, it was a different era. Hard to believe it was even the same lifetime.

11

When the official 1958 World Cup games got under way, Garrincha and I both found ourselves stuck in the same place—on the bench. Some of the team managers believed Garrincha was too mentally undisciplined to play against our first opponent, Austria, whose strategy was based on impressive tactical precision on the attack. As for me, my problem remained my knee. Dr. Gosling told me that, to have any hope of playing, I'd need to undertake a series of very painful treatments. They mostly involved placing burning hot towels on my knee. Remember, this was presumably one of the best sports medicine doctors in the world—which is to say, the world was still in the dark ages. But I obliged, without complaint. I desperately wanted to get on the field.

In the first match, Brazil played wonderfully, beating the Austrians 3–0 behind two goals from Mazzola and one from Nilton Santos, whose performance was apparently unaffected by the contraband he'd purchased. But in our second game, against England, the team came out flat and we played them to that most dreaded of soccer results—the 0–0 tie. In the "group play" format used in Sweden, and in all future

World Cups, the initial games took place among four teams, with the top two teams moving on to an elimination round. After only managing a tie against England, we'd need to beat our third and final opponent to be sure of advancing.

When I learned we might be just one game away from going home, I thought I was going to lose my mind. Why wasn't my knee getting better?

Thankfully, the veteran players helped to reassure me, especially Waldyr Pereira, known as "Didi," who always showed a quiet and kind of eerily unshakable faith in my ability, even then. At thirty, he was one of the oldest players among us—so old, by the strange calculus of professional athletics, that the team's management had almost left him behind in Brazil, thinking him past his prime. But Didi's experience and demeanor were precisely what our excitable group of novices needed—he was so cool, unruffled and poised that many people compared him to a jazz musician. Another one of his nicknames was "The Ethiopian Prince"—which was far cooler, by, like, a million degrees, than "Pelé." And I'll always be grateful to Didi for, among his many, many feats at the 1958 World Cup, helping me to keep my feet on the ground when I was still hurt.

"Your moment will come, kid," he'd say, patting me on the back, like I shouldn't have a care in the world. "Just relax and keep the weight off that knee!"

It was sound advice. I went to see Dr. Gosling again, and did a series of drills while he watched. He didn't say much, but I could tell it went well. The day before the game, Zito, my teammate from Santos, came up to me and said: "I think the moment has come for us." I didn't quite believe him. But a short time later, one of the heads of the delegation came over to me, put his hand on my shoulder, and said:

"Are you ready, Pelé?"

The smile I gave him was a thousand miles wide. Soon, I learned the team officials, believing we needed a spark, had finally dropped whatever reservations they had about Garrincha. He was going to play in the upcoming match, too. Then it was just a question of preparing for our next opponent. Boy, was it a doozy.

12

In 1958, there was one country that cultivated an aura of mystery above all others: the Soviet Union. This was *especially* true on the soccer field. We were at the height of the Cold War, and the Soviets were determined to convince the world that their system—Communism—was superior to all others in every aspect of life. Just one year earlier, in a display of their scientific and military might, the Soviets had put Sputnik, the first satellite ever, into space. Now, with a victory at the World Cup, they would show us that they were the best in sport as well.

One thing that has always fascinated me about soccer, even today, is the way that national teams often reflect national characteristics. You can tell a lot about a country by the way they play the game. For example, the Germans were always known for having "efficient" teams that didn't waste a single pass or dribble. One English writer, Brian Glanville, said of his nation's team: "England, in conformity with the English character, have always combined disciplined solidity with occasional eccentric genius." Of course, when talking about such things, it's important not to get too carried away with stereotypes. But a lot has also been said, quite rightly I think, about how the Brazilian style of play also reflects our national character: full of joy, improvisation, and our willingness, for better and for worse, to ignore established conventions and rules. Some observers even saw traces of our ethnic makeup—the famed Brazilian sociologist Gilberto Freyre wrote in 1938 that the qualities of "surprise, cunning, astuteness, fleetness and . . . individual brilliance and spontaneity" that Brazilian teams displayed on the soccer field were a reflection of our "mulatto spirit."

In that vein, the Soviets called their style of play "scientific soccer," reflecting their belief that the same qualities that had put Sputnik into space could get them a World Cup championship as well. They had taken data, training and an emphasis on mental acuity to a level that our Brazilian officials, with their pulled teeth and behavioral tests, could only fantasize about. Unlike us, the Soviet approach had already obtained real results—including a gold medal in soccer at the most recent Olympics, the 1956 games in Melbourne, Australia. Stories about the Soviets' meticulous preparations echoed throughout the other teams' camps. We heard their players were capable of running at full speed for three hours without stopping. Someone told us that they even did four hours of gymnastics on the mornings of their games.

Of course, some of this was just Cold War propaganda—but we didn't know this at the time. This was an era before teams could scout their opponents by watching film or video; all we could rely on was word of mouth. And so, we were convinced that we were about to face a race of bona fide super-beings, bigger and perhaps smarter than us in every possible way.

The intimidating face of the Soviet team was its goalie, Lev Yashin—and in his case, much of the hype was very much grounded in fact. At six-foot-two, Yashin towered over other players on the field, and he spent entire games screaming orders at everyone, friend and foe alike. He was tough in a particularly Soviet way, having started his soccer career while still a teenager during World War II, when he was sent to work at a military factory in Moscow and began playing for its in-house team. He was also an excellent goalie in ice hockey. Yashin was known as "The Black Spider"—partly because of his habit of dressing in all black clothes, and also because he made so many impossible saves that it often seemed as if he possessed eight arms. He was not just a product of propaganda; he was truly one of the all-time greats. In 2013, a panel of experts in the magazine *World Soccer* overwhelmingly voted Yashin the best goalkeeper of all time.

If this was indeed a matchup of national personalities, then how could the joy and improvisational skills of a poor country like Brazil possibly triumph over the training, planning and wealth of a superpower like the Soviet Union?

Well, our coaches had an answer: by kicking them in the face. Not literally, of course. But they did believe that, from the moment the game started, the Brazilian team needed to do something dramatic to disorient the Soviets to get them out of their comfort zone. If we could get the game out of the realm of science, and into the realm of human behavior, then we might just have a chance at victory.

13

A s I ran out onto the field in Gothenburg, and stripped off my warm-up gear, I swear I heard gasps from the fifty-five thousand people in attendance. I was still so small and baby-faced that many fans probably believed I was just the team mascot. I walked over to the bench, and Mário Américo, the trainer, gave me one last massage on my knee.

"Looks good," he said. "You're going on now, kid."

I don't remember being that nervous—I had lots of adrenaline, sure, but I was mostly just excited to finally be back out on the field. Soccer, as always, was the easy part.

As Garrincha and I took our positions, I saw a few confused looks on the faces of the Soviets. Our team had gone to great lengths to disguise the fact that the two of us would be playing. We'd heard there was a Soviet spy tracking our movements, so the team had abruptly switched the time of our final practice, when Garrincha and I played with the starters for the first time. Brazil could play Cold War games too! Apparently our subterfuge had worked. Before the Soviets could realize what was going on, the whistle blew, and the game was under way.

What followed was a flurry of action unlike anything I've ever been a part of since. Garrincha quickly got the ball and started making his way up the right wing, juking and pausing with seemingly every single step. His beautiful, twisted legs confused the hell out of opponents and made him absolutely impossible to defend—because of their strange angles, defenders could never tell which way Garrincha was going to turn next. Plus, being a natural jokester, he took special delight in fooling, and sometimes even taunting his opponents with his bizarre, circus-style moves. Virtually from the first moment Garrincha touched the ball that day, I could hear people in the crowd laughing. The stands were filled almost entirely with Swedes, but thanks largely to his antics, they were cheering for Brazil from the get-go. The Soviets, meanwhile, were utterly bewildered—nothing in their scientific manuals had prepared them for this!

Garrincha beat a final defender and launched a wicked shot on goal. Unfortunately, it ricocheted off the crossbar. Just a few moments later, the ball came rolling over to me. I summoned all my strength, took aim at the net and—

Clang!

Another ball off the crossbar! I must have looked heartbroken, because Didi, once again possessing enough poise for all of us, yelled from across the field:

"Relax, kid, the goal will come!"

He was right. Almost immediately, Didi himself found an opening and put a beautiful pass through to Vavá, one of our forwards, who duly smashed the ball into the net.

Brazil 1, Soviet Union 0.

It's hard to believe, but after that rush of action and emotion, the game was still only three minutes old. Gabriel Hanot, a French journalist who had covered the sport for decades, later described them as "the finest three minutes in the history of soccer."

Inevitably, we slowed down a bit after that. But the rhythm of the game had been established, and the Soviets never really recovered their composure. I gave an assist to another goal by Vavá in the second half that provided us with our final result: Brazil 2, Soviet Union 0. The score could have been even more tilted in our favor had it not been for Yashin, the Black Spider, who made plenty of excellent saves that day.

The real revelation, of course, was the player who would henceforth be known in Brazil as *O Anjo de Pernas Tortas*—"The Angel with Bent Legs." Thanks largely to him, we were through to the quarterfinals, and a matchup against Wales that would take place later that week in the exact same stadium.

"Congratulations, Gothenburg," one Swedish newspaper proclaimed. "On Thursday, you'll get to see Garrincha again!"

14

Our victory over the mighty Soviets had another effect: It was the game that convinced people back in Brazil that maybe, just maybe, it was OK to start believing in their national team again. All the despair of 1950, and the apathy of 1954, started to finally thaw, as if the clouds had parted after a long winter and the sun was finally shining on Brazilian soccer again. Radios flipped back on; newspapers began to fly off the stands. Our fans began daring to dream once more of that elusive first world championship.

Our performance was important, but Brazilians were also feeling better about themselves in general. Soccer wasn't the only good thing happening in our country in 1958. That was also the same year that João Gilberto recorded his album *Chega de Saudade*, which helped launch a brand-new musical genre: the bossa nova. The album's most popular track, "The Girl from Ipanema," would become one of the most famous songs of all time. Bossa nova joined soccer as the face of Brazil in the world—and was an even bigger source of pride in some ways, because it was something totally and uniquely Brazilian that we had invented ourselves.

In coming years, I'd get to spend some time with João, and despite his reputation for being a slightly difficult personality, he always graciously indulged me in my somewhat amateurish passion for music. We met at several events in Brazil and in New York City, and I always found him refreshingly direct. I do have one regret though—I never got to play music with him. I might not be the world's best musician, but I did pick up guitar over the years and I loved to sing. What I lacked in talent, I made up for in passion, and I got to play over the years with other Brazilian music giants like Tom Jobim, Sérgio Mendes and Roberto Carlos. Heck, I even got to sing with Frank Sinatra once! But I never got to play with João, even though I greatly respected what he did and felt a certain kinship with him. We were part of two victorious generations who would promote Brazil for decades to come.

In the late 1950s, even our politics seemed to be going pretty well—the president was Juscelino Kubitschek, an easygoing and competent man whom some called "the bossa nova president." Juscelino—who like many Brazilian presidents was known by his first name—was determined to make Brazil a modern and prosperous country as quickly as he possibly could. He called his development plan "Fifty years of progress in five," with a focus on building up Brazilian industries. Suddenly, we were producing kitchen appliances, sewing machines and other goods that other countries took for granted, but had never been widely available in the tropics before. Auto factories began to pop up in greater São Paulo, and soon, Brazil would begin its passionate love affair with cars.

Juscelino's biggest and most ambitious project was to build a new capital from scratch—Brasilia. The city would be located on a stretch of arid high plains right on the border of the state where I was born, Minas Gerais. The idea was that, by forcing the politicians to leave Rio and live in the interior, maybe they'd start paying a little more attention to places like Baurú and Três Corações, and maybe some money would even fall out of their pockets for the humble folk. Up until that point, Brazil's biggest cities were concentrated almost entirely along the ocean—"like crabs clinging to the coast," to use one famous phrase. Juscelino, being the impatient sort, wanted the city finished by 1960. There had never really been an undertaking like this in modern history—at the exact moment we were playing in Sweden, thousands of construction workers were busily erecting the ministries and palaces that would soon form one of the world's most unique cities. It was another achievement that seemed to indicate that Brazil had left its poor, backward, obscure past behind.

Brazil was, in short, a country fully primed for a giant leap—a transformation. All we had to do was keep the ball rolling.

15

The Welsh, being the clever sort, came to their match against us with one overriding objective—not to let Garrincha beat them.

After his extraordinary display against the Soviets, it was a pretty good strategy. Throughout that game, Garrincha had at least two, and sometimes three defenders shadowing him at all times. Not even he, with his transcendent talent, was able to work his magic while being so thoroughly smothered.

The obvious drawback to triple-teaming anybody was that it opened up opportunities for other players. But that Welsh team was very good, with a stout defense and a widely respected and beloved coach, Jimmy Murphy. In group play, they had soundly beaten Hungary, which had sent us home in the 1954 World Cup and ultimately placed second in that tournament. Were the Welsh from a relatively small nation? Yes. But for goodness' sake, the last team on earth that was going to underestimate a small-country opponent in 1958 was Brazil!

The first half ended scoreless. I didn't really get many chances with the ball. But Didi later said that he had been "saving" me during the first forty-five minutes of the game. He believed that because of my age, no one would really pay attention to me—they might even forget about me entirely. I was a boy no one needed to fear; and sure enough, the defenders' attention seemed to fade as the game went on. Didi was like a great conductor, and I was the young soloist whose moment was yet to come.

With twenty minutes left in the game, my moment finally arrived. Garrincha, for maybe the first time all game, had only one defender on him. He took advantage of the opening and passed to Didi, who passed the ball to me. I had my back to the goal, and Didi was still running, expecting me to give it back to him. But instead, I reacted instinctively, just as Dondinho had always taught me. I "caught" the ball with my chest, and then, without letting it touch the ground, I looped it over the outstretched foot of a Welsh defender—"cheekily," one announcer said. The ball bounced once, and I nimbly stepped around the defender and rifled it home into the bottom left-hand corner of the goal.

Brazil 1, Wales 0.

I screamed—a long, guttural roar. I ran toward the goal and jumped for joy, once, twice, and then fell on my knees to pull the ball out of the back of the net.

Four of my teammates came running into the goal and swarmed me, knocking me down and pinning me to the ground. After them came a dozen or so news photographers—they raced onto the field itself, which they really weren't supposed to do, but oh well! They began taking shots of us rolling around on the ground. Finally, one of the Welsh players came in, somewhat grouchily, and started trying to pull us off of one another, as if to say—All right, guys, that's enough.

I really wasn't trying to gloat, or show anybody up. The honest truth is, I was paralyzed with happiness. I just couldn't stop screaming and laughing. I felt like something within me had been awakened—never to sleep again.

16

That goal provided us with our final margin against Wales—the slimmest of victories, 1–0. After the game, I remember getting hugs from teammates, and some congratulations from members of the press. But after that, everything became kind of a blur. I had become caught up in something much bigger than I was, and rather than fight it, I let myself get swept away.

I've always dreamed of soccer—what else?—and during those days and nights after the Wales victory I would drift away to fantasies the likes of which I'd never had before. Each dribble, each pass, each shot now spawned many different possibilities. I'd dream of passing the ball left instead of right, juking a final defender instead of taking a shot far from goal. Now that I knew for certain I could score a goal on the world stage, more possibilities seemed to open up—instead of three variations on a single play, I could now see ten. And the goal itself seemed a hundred yards wide.

I'd wake up with a start—wide-awake and utterly happy, ready to take the field, and ready to make these dreams a reality.

17

Before I knew it, I was on the field once again—this time against France, in the World Cup semifinal.

I was quiet once again in the first half, which ended with us up 2–1—a tenuous lead. Echoing the previous match, Didi virtually ignored me for the first forty-five minutes. But I didn't despair—I knew the pattern by now. And indeed, after halftime, things started to open up.

Seven minutes after the second half started, a very ripe-looking ball came rolling across the face of the goal. The French goalkeeper, Claude Abbes, couldn't hold on to it, and when the ball squirmed from his grasp, I knocked it into the empty net for my first goal of the game. I couldn't miss. It was one of the easiest goals I'd ever score.

Brazil 3, France 1.

Ten minutes later, in the game's sixty-fourth minute, Garrincha nearly dribbled out of bounds on our opponent's side before cutting the ball back to me. I brought the ball down and got it past an oncoming French defender, and then passed it on. The ball bounced around a bit, before rolling back over to me about eight yards from the goal. I then rifled the ball in for my second goal.

Brazil 4, France 1.

After another ten minutes, with seventy-five of the game's ninety-plus minutes now gone, I received yet another brilliant pass from—who else? Garrincha. From just outside the penalty box, on the right side of the field, he passed it over to me. I was about twelve yards out, and pretty well covered, but I was able to create just a little bit of space and knock the ball into the bottom left-hand corner of the net for my third goal of the game—a hat trick, in just one half of play.

Brazil 5, France 1.

By the end of the game, the crowd was going absolutely crazy. Even after the French scored a last-minute goal to make the final score 5–2, people inside the stadium continued to clap, laugh and shout my name. "Pelé! Pelé!" The atmosphere was one of delight and discovery—as if something new and unexpected had come into the world.

The Swedish crowd was so effusive that I felt like I was back in Brazil. This was very generous of them, especially since by that point some people in the stadium must have known the truth—we'd be playing the host team in the final.

18

I t was only fitting that, before we could raise the Cup, we had to stare down the Ghost of 1950 one last time.

Our opponent in the final was, indeed, the host country: Sweden. This presented an unexpected problem. Both Brazil and Sweden had, up to that point in the 1958 tournament, been using yellow jerseys. One of us would have to give them up for the final. The Brazilian delegation thought the Swedish should be the gracious hosts, and let the visiting team—us—use our preferred jersey. But it was not to be. The Swedes decided to resolve the issue with a coin flip, which they promptly won.

No problem, our team leaders thought. After all, the Brazilian flag had several other colors, providing several other options—white, green, or blue. So the directors announced at a team meeting they had chosen white.

A very neutral, safe color, right?

Wrong.

White was the color that the Brazilian team wore during the final against Uruguay at the Maracanã in 1950.

All the players looked at one another, wide-eyed. This was lunacy! The room got very quiet. Finally, the team directors realized their mistake, and Dr. Paulo Machado abruptly declared we'd be wearing blue instead. When this failed to noticeably lift our spirits, Dr. Machado pointed out that blue was also the color of Brazil's patron saint: Our Lady of Aparecida. This revelation met with some oohs and ahhs from the players—thus, the matter was considered closed.

Teams nowadays play with multimillion-dollar operating budgets, numerous corporate sponsors, and enough uniforms and shoes to comfortably dress a small army. But in 1958, there was still precious little money in professional soccer. As a result, the sudden change in uniforms presented us with another dilemma—we had run out of shirts! Sure, we had brought some blue ones with us, but we had worn them a lot during our practices. They were all tattered and faded now—not exactly worthy of the pageantry of a World Cup final. So two of our team officials, Adolpho Marques and the dentist Mário Trigo, took it upon themselves to go into downtown Stockholm to buy us some shiny, brand-new shirts from a Swedish department store. Mário Américo—the same kindly therapist who had looked after my knee—then spent the whole Saturday morning before the game painstakingly removing our numbers and logos from the yellow shirts one by one and sewing them back onto the new blue ones.

With that emergency resolved, everything else seemed like a piece of cake.

19

When I woke up on the morning of the final—June 28, 1958—you'd think I would have been feeling unbearable pressure. But Didi and all the veterans had done a great job of keeping all of us loose, and by that point we knew our team was blessed with a great combination of experience and talent. The team management's methodical approach of shielding us from the outside world had also worked pretty well, in the end—we had precious little exposure to the histrionics playing out in the press back home. In fact, we were so sheltered that Garrincha acted as if he was shocked to learn this would be our final game. In the Rio de Janeiro state tournament, which Garrincha played in with his club team back home, you got to play each opponent twice. In the World Cup, of course, it was now just one final game—for all the marbles.

"Really?" he said incredulously. "What a boring tournament!"

I'm pretty sure Garrincha was just joking around. But when we arrived at the stadium later that day in Solna, a suburb of Stockholm, we were all still cracking up.

OK, we had *some* nerves. They were evidenced by a number of sloppy passes and turnovers by our team right after the opening whistle. Sweden quickly took advantage of our mistakes and scored first—putting them up 1–0 in just the fourth minute of the game. I guess this could have rattled us—it was, in fact, the first time our team had trailed in the entire tournament. And the Swedish home crowd was going crazy, literally throwing their hats into the air.

But, like I said, we had acquired this new, almost eerie confidence—and the same fantastic leadership that had brought us to that point wasn't going to buckle now. After that first Swedish goal, it was Didi—of course—who picked up the ball and walked *very* slowly with it back to midfield, speaking very calmly to each Brazilian player he passed along the way. "Very good, that's over!" Didi said cheerily. "Time for us now!"

Indeed, just five minutes later, Garrincha got loose on the right-hand side of the field, pulling the Swedish goalie out of position. He passed it over to Vavá, who scored the tying goal. In the thirty-second minute of the first half, I got free and passed the ball to Garrincha, who found Vavá once again. That gave us a 2–1 lead going into halftime.

Shortly after the second half began, I scored one of the most well-known goals of my career. I called to Nilton Santos to make a long pass from across the field. I caught the ball with my chest, then let it drop as a Swedish player ran toward me. With a flick of my foot, I then flipped the ball right over the defender's head. It was pure street ball, the kind of move that we had practiced a million times back at "Rubens Arruda Stadium" in Baurú. Perhaps only a seventeen-year-old would have had the sheer audacity to try such a move in a World Cup final. I ran around the defender and volleyed it home from about ten yards out, making it Brazil 3, Sweden 1.

After that goal, a strange thing happened: We won over the Swedish crowd. Even though they were surely disappointed to see their own team losing, some of them began chanting "Samba! Samba!" They applauded our moves, oohed and ahhed as we passed the ball around, and cheered wildly when we scored our fourth goal. It was truly remarkable, the sportsmanship and love for good soccer that they showed that day. I have to say, in all the years since, I have never seen a more gracious, fair audience.

As the final minutes of the game ticked away, and we retained our insurmountable lead, I finally started to comprehend what was happening. Brazil was going to be the world champion! After nearly thirty years of disappointments, of near misses and national trauma, we would now get that elusive first title. This was amazing, a real honor. But what really got me emotional, as I continued to run around the field and try to keep my Swedish opponent in check, was the thought of my mom and dad back home in Baurú. All our family and friends would be there in our house, laughing and cheering around the radio, just like they had in 1950. Except this time, they'd get to celebrate! Instead of tears, there would be laughter! And they would be cheering my name!

These thoughts, which I'd been able to suppress until that moment, were too much for me to bear. With each step, I felt my feet getting lighter and lighter. And on the game's very final play, I guess I just kind of snapped. A ball came looping over from the side of the field. I soared into the air, timing my leap perfectly. I kept my eyes wide open, just as Dad had spent all those hours teaching me back in Baurú, during all those silly drills. And as the ball went in—a goal worthy of Dondinho, a header, his specialty—everything just faded to black.

I passed out. Right there on the field, directly in front of the goal.

Mercifully, the referee blew the whistle, declaring the game over, and Brazil the world champions. My header had made the final score Brazil 5, Sweden 2.

I lay there, without moving, for a good while. Garrincha, sweet soul that he was, was the first player to run over to help me. He lifted up my legs, thinking this might somehow send blood back to my head.

When I regained consciousness, there was sheer pandemonium. I saw my teammates laughing, hugging, and jumping up and down. Hundreds of people had run onto the field to celebrate with us. I stood up, saw Didi and Garrincha, and then the tears began to roll down my face. I've always been a real crybaby—surely you've figured this out by now—but never in my life did the tears come as freely as they did at that moment. I was overwhelmed with thoughts of my family, my country, and the sheer release that came with finally being able to let my emotions go. I continued to sob, utterly inconsolable, on the shoulders of my teammates as people kept pouring out of the stands. Reporters, fans and police were all grabbing me, patting me on the back and on the head, smiling ear to ear and yelling things in languages I couldn't understand.

My knees collapsed again, and I began to fall to the ground. Then I realized I was being lifted, as if by some kind of invisible force. It was my teammates, putting me on their shoulders and parading me around the field as I wept and wept.

Gylmar reached up, squeezed my leg and smiled.

"Go ahead and cry, boy! It's good for you!"

Somebody grabbed a Swedish flag, and then we paraded that around the field in honor of our amazing hosts. When my teammates put me back down, I ran around the grass, screaming and laughing and crying, shouting at anybody who would listen: "I've got to tell my dad! I've got to tell my dad!"

20

Of course, there was no Skype in 1958—and no cell phones either. So I'd have to wait three whole days to tell Dad all about our adventure in Sweden.

The euphoria of the game melded seamlessly into a drawn-out, days-long celebration. While we were still on the field, the Swedish monarch, King Gustaf, came down to shake our hands and congratulate us. He was very dignified and gracious—just as all the Swedes had been. Even the Swedish players were generous in their praise after the game. The defender who had been charged with covering me, Sigge Parling, told the press: "After the fifth goal, even I wanted to cheer for him."

That night, we had a huge meal at our hotel, where we stuffed ourselves and some people drank champagne from the Jules Rimet trophy, named for the FIFA president who had organized the first Cup back in 1930. When the time finally came for us to fly back home, our first stop on Brazilian soil was Recife, where thousands of people had come to greet us a few weeks earlier. This time, of course, the crowd was much larger—despite a driving tropical rain. As soon as the plane's doors opened, the crowd erupted in cheers. We came out, and they lifted us up on their shoulders.

When we landed in Rio later that day, the crowd went mad with joy. We were exhausted by this point—none of us had really slept since the night before the game—but there was no way to stop now. The streets were packed with people. They paraded us around on fire engines. People dropped firecrackers, shredded newspapers, pretty much anything they could find out of office and apartment windows. Then the team officials whisked us back to a local magazine's office where, to our surprise, our families were waiting for us.

Dondinho and Dona Celeste were standing there, smiling with pride. Both of them were trying to keep a stiff upper lip and control their emotions with so many people watching. Did they succeed? Well, let's just say that my genes came from somewhere!

"Everybody is so proud of you, Dico!" my mom said, gasping the words, tears rolling down her cheeks. "Even your teachers—they all came to see me and say how they always knew you would be such a success."

That was the most ridiculous thing I'd ever heard! But it was a great moment for my family—I saw that my mom now understood all the good that soccer could bring us.

There was a party at the presidential palace, where Juscelino himself drank champagne from the Cup. From there, it was on to São Paulo for yet another parade and celebration. After a quick stopover in Santos, I was finally allowed to go back to Baurú.

By this point, I was hoping that I just would be able to go home and rest. Fat chance! The atmosphere in my hometown was just as crazy as it had been in São Paulo or Rio, with one major difference—here, the celebration was focused entirely upon me. As our plane touched down at the Baurú airstrip—the same one I'd visited so many times over the years, and where I'd seen the wrecked glider way back when— I could see that literally the entire town had turned out to see us. Hordes of people were pressed up against the fences on the side of the runway, waving and cheering.

I stepped out of the plane, smiled and waved. It was hard to believe that I was the same kid who, just two years earlier, had donned long pants and boarded a bus for Santos, his knees knocking in fear. My past and present felt like a dream—both equally unreal. But all the usual suspects were there—my friends from the street, my brother and sister, my parents. Even the mayor had turned out to give me a big hug.

"Baurú has been waiting for you, Pelé!" he declared.

I couldn't believe my eyes. The mayor motioned for me to board a flatbed truck for yet another victory parade, which ended at a stand in the main square. I was given trophies, medals and gifts, as the crowd laughed and applauded. One of the medals was supposed to be presented by my mom. But she was too overwhelmed with emotions, so she just walked up onstage and gave me a tender kiss on the cheek.

Two of the gifts I received were particularly memorable. One was a new car—a Romi-Isetta. It was a little wisp of a vehicle, with just three wheels, but having any automobile was an enormously big deal in Brazil at that time. The total price for an imported American car was about twenty thousand dollars; this in a country where the average minimum wage was about thirty dollars a month. I was honored. There was one slight catch: I was a minor, so I couldn't actually drive it! There was also some doubt about whether the thing was sturdy enough to make it all the way down to Santos. So I gave the car to Dondinho.

The funniest gift of all was actually a television—a big green and yellow monstrosity, painted with the colors of Brazil, that had been presented to us while we were still in Sweden. The dilemma with the TV was similar to the one with the car—in Baurú, as in most of Brazil, there was still no working broadcast signal. So it turned into a kind of trophy; one that I still have in my home near Santos today.

All these gifts, and all the celebration, had another effect: They began to create the impression that I was rich. Once the celebration was over, and I went back with my family to spend a few quiet days at our house, our doorbell never stopped ringing. Old friends and other people were suddenly asking for money or favors; whether I had any resources for business ideas; and so on. In truth, there was hardly any new money to speak of—I would continue to play for Santos at the same salary as before.

Nonetheless, nobody believed me when I said I didn't have any cash. After all, I was on the front pages of newspapers and magazines all over the world. One of the world's most famous magazines, *Paris Match,* ran a cover story about me, declaring that there was a new king of soccer. After that, people in Brazil started calling me *O Rei*—the King. Many people assumed I was living like one, too.

I felt overwhelmed. The world had changed, but I felt like I hadn't. I was just a kid who loved playing soccer. I had discovered my true talent, and I had gone where it led me. I'd had some success. I'd had the honor of winning a championship for my country. But I didn't understand why everybody now seemed to *want* something from me— not just cash, but words of encouragement or a favor for a nephew. Some people only seemed to want to give me things! It was crazy. I tried to smile as big as I could, and make people happy with my answers to their questions. But, during those first days in Baurú, I began to realize that people were constantly watching, and that my life was no longer my own. That feeling has been with me ever since.

21

All these years later, I still smile when I think about that 1958 team. We had something truly special: a collection of phenomenal individual talents who played with total abandon. We were almost too young, too innocent to realize the scale of what we were doing. That first game against the Soviets signaled the beginning of one of the most remarkable streaks in professional sports: For the following eight years, whenever Garrincha and I were on the field together playing for Brazil, our team never lost a single game.

Eleven members of the 1958 team, including myself and Garrincha, would go on to play in the next World Cup, which took place in Chile in 1962. Once again, I got hurt, in just the second game, and I missed the rest of the tournament. But history would also repeat itself in far more pleasant ways: Brazil won that 1962 Cup, giving us back-to-back titles. That tournament is remembered in Brazil, quite rightly, as Garrincha's championship.

Life would get more complicated in coming years—things would never again be quite as simple, or quite as pure, as they were in 1958.

But there was always one thing that would make my worries melt away.

A few days after returning home to Baurú from the World Cup in Sweden, I happened to walk past one of the places where the Sete de Setembro crew used to play. There were a bunch of boys of about eight or ten years old, kicking the ball around, laughing and having fun, just like my friends and I used to do. I asked if I could join them, and they said yes.

So I went home, changed out of my long pants, and put on some shorts. When I got back to the field, I removed my shoes, and played barefoot, just like they were. All of us played together for hours, until the sun went down, and our mothers called us home. Just a couple of boys from Baurú.

MEXICO, 1970

1

called the reporters over to my locker, and said I had an announcement to make.

"I will never play in another World Cup," I declared. "If soccer means war, then I will hang my shoes on the wall, and forget that I ever played."

The date was July 19, 1966—eight years after that first championship in Sweden. The place was Liverpool, England. I was still only twenty-five years old—not exactly retirement age. But I felt about fifty years old that day because of the pain in my body, and the deep scars and bruises on my legs. Indeed, it felt like I'd been to war—and lost. Although I would continue to play club soccer for Santos, I announced that I was done forever with the Brazilian national team.

"That's it," I said, as the reporters gaped at me, scribbling furiously. "This is the last time you'll see me in the uniform of Brazil."

Making a major decision like that in the heat of the moment is never a good idea. In fact, it was downright dumb. But I had never been so furious, so disappointed, and so fed up with soccer as I was that day.

If only I could somehow go back in time and talk to that twenty-five-year-old guy! I'd tell him to relax a little bit, and stop being so dramatic! I'd tell him things are never quite as bad as they seem after a big defeat. I'd tell him some adversity can make your life worthwhile, and make your triumphs even sweeter.

Above all, I'd tell him that there were still some things that even Pelé, the so-called "king" of soccer, hadn't learned yet. Including maybe the most important of all the lessons that soccer has to teach.

2

In the months prior to that day in Liverpool, I had been having a recurring dream—a fantastic, deeply satisfying dream. In it, I was standing on the field at Wembley Stadium, the grand palace of soccer in England—one of the few major global venues I'd never played in before. Everybody on the Brazilian national team was there with me: exhausted, sweaty, but happy. And we were about to be presented the Jules Rimet Cup by Queen Elizabeth II herself, in celebration of yet another world championship—our third, an unprecedented feat.

Just as the queen was about to hand us the trophy, I'd wake up with a start. I'd lie there happy for a moment, certain the dream was going to become reality. And then I'd jump out of bed and go train for hours, just to make sure it did.

Unfortunately, I wasn't the only one having such delusions. Throughout Brazil, many people were treating the 1966 World Cup like a victory lap, rather than the kind of prize you had to work hard for. After our consecutive titles of 1958 and 1962, many of our Brazilian coaches and players seemed to think we would just fly over to England, drink some tea, kick the ball around a bit and collect the trophy, thank you very much. Newspapers were full of stories about our impending triumph, and how our soccer prowess showed that Brazilians were superior in every way. And if you're thinking that sounds a lot like the attitude that got us into trouble at the Maracanã in 1950, you're exactly right. I guess two championships had allowed Brazil to fall back into some of its old bad habits.

In fact, some of the coincidences were eerie. The insecurity of our politicians was helping to drive the hype once again. All the optimism of the late 1950s, the years of President Juscelino Kubitschek and our great triumph in Sweden, had suddenly come crashing down. It was just the latest cycle of great hope followed by great disappointment that, sadly, has always seemed to define politics in Brazil.

Juscelino's "Fifty years of progress in five" plan did succeed in getting lots of new roads and factories built, as he had promised. Our glorious new capital, Brasilia, opened as planned in 1960. But there are no miracles in this world, and the construction binge seemed to create as many new problems for Brazil as it solved. The government printed a bunch of money to pay for all these projects, and Brazilians began to darkly joke that now we had "Fifty years of inflation in five." Every time you went to the supermarket, or out to eat, the bill seemed to rise. In 1964, prices doubled in just one year, making people furious.

Meanwhile, there was another issue complicating things—it was the sixties! Seemingly everywhere in the world, it was a turbulent time of protests, strikes, revolutions and free love. This was just as true in Brazil—and not only the free love part. Poor Brazilians were moving out of farms and small towns like Três Corações and into the big cities, hoping they'd find a better life for themselves and their kids, but usually having to settle for *favelas* on the hills and precarious riverbanks of places like Rio and São Paulo. Meanwhile, young people were demanding greater freedoms, and a bigger slice of the pie for themselves.

All of these demands would have been tough on any politician. But Juscelino's successors didn't seem up to the challenge. One of them resigned, got drunk and boarded a boat for Europe after just eight months on the job. That left behind his vice president, a guy named João "Jango" Goulart, who seemed nice enough when we met him in

Brasilia to celebrate the World Cup title of 1962. But as time went by, Jango appointed some communist advisers and began speaking of redistributing land to the poor in Brazil's cities. That didn't sit very well with the elite. In 1964, the military staged a coup, and Brazil became a conservative dictatorship once again.

As I've said, soccer is never immune from such things—especially not in Brazil. As we began preparing for the World Cup of 1966, we were under tremendous pressure from a new military government that desperately wanted us to help them cover up the turbulent divisions in our society. The soldiers understood, all too well, that soccer unites like nothing else can. They believed that a third consecutive championship was the key to getting life in Brazil back to "normal" once again—and maybe even turning back the clock to the simpler, less demanding era of the 1950s.

Am I getting carried away? Does it seem like I'm blaming our politicians for *everything*? OK, fair enough—after all, it is the players who take the field, and ultimately win or lose the games. But consider some of the decisions the Brazilian soccer team managers made that year, some of which were so bizarre that they could be explained only by the crazy politics of the mid-1960s. For example, instead of inviting twenty-two or twenty-eight players to try out for the Brazilian team, as was customary, that year our managers invited forty-four players! This was amazing. Why on earth would they do such a thing? Well, they divided us into four separate squads of eleven each. Then they separately sent each squad to cities and towns all over the country to "practice"—to big metropolises like São Paulo and Belo Horizonte, as well as smaller locales like Três Rios, Caxambú and Teresópolis. Practicing separately, and rotating towns every few days, did absolutely nothing to prepare us for the World Cup. But that wasn't the point. We were there primarily to entertain, to unite, to dish out favors to local politicians, and to make people forget about the country's problems. We were the classic "bread and circus."

Following that sideshow, the team officials—again, more concerned with projecting a happy face to the world than actually getting us ready to play—scheduled an exhausting series of warm-up matches for us in Spain, Scotland, Sweden and elsewhere. The games took place in a variety of different climates and with lots of travel days in between. When it came time for us to leave for Europe, we didn't yet have a team—we had a massive, somewhat awkward collection of individuals. Sure, some of the names were the same: Garrincha was still there, as were Gylmar and Djalma Santos. But eight years had passed since Sweden, an eternity in sports. Everybody was older, and not always able to still perform at soccer's highest level.

Even when all the players were finally together, the coaches couldn't decide on a starting lineup. The same group never played together twice, and sometimes we'd change five, six or seven starters from one game to the next—an unforgiveable sin, especially at the World Cup level. When we could manage only a 1–1 tie against Scotland, I think panic began to set in. None of our dreams of Wembley or the queen were going to come true with us playing that way. There was quite a bit of finger-pointing among the players after that game, and lots of anger. The older guys on the team—Nilton Santos, Zito and Bellini, the captain—went to the team managers and said we needed to all get in a room and talk things out.

The managers agreed. But when the meeting finally took place, it was a one-sided affair. In the political and social climate of those years, in Brazil as in many other countries, anyone in a position of authority acted as if their voice was the only one that mattered. The word of our managers and bosses simply could not be questioned. So, even though it was a team meeting, the managers did all the talking that day. They told us, somewhat testily, that everything would be fine: All we had to do was win a few more games in England and then we'd go home and be honored as champions once again, so could we all please stop the complaining?

I remember walking out of that meeting and looking over at Garrincha. He shook his head, sadly. I just shrugged. Neither of us said a word. This was itself a sign of things to come—and the lessons I still had to learn. But we didn't know that then, so we just quietly packed our bags. Like lambs to the slaughter, off we went to England.

3

From the first second of our first game, we realized we had more than our own internal problems to deal with.

At the previous two World Cups, Brazil had dazzled the world with our flamboyant, wide-open, constantly attacking style of play. Now, in England, we heard the referees were going to try to level the playing field. They were going to be more tolerant of physical defense and call far fewer fouls. This was a change that would favor the Europeans, who were generally bigger and stronger than the South American players, and had spent the last eight years devising techniques to disrupt our attack. Lest this sound like yet another conspiracy theory, or perhaps sour grapes on my part, I'm not the only person who thought the South American teams got a raw deal in 1966. Antonio Rattin, the number ten for the Argentine team that year, decades later was still calling it "the most violent World Cup of all time." Brian Viner, an English journalist, wrote in *The Independent* of London in 2009 that "several players (for Brazil), but Pelé in particular, suffered some of the most egregiously vindictive man-marking ever seen."

Now, I never shied away from physical play. We used to beat the living tar out of one another on the streets of Baurú! Once my professional career began, I was usually the highest scorer on the field—and, let's be honest, everybody wanted to say they shut down Pelé. Defenses targeted me and assigned one and sometimes two or even three defenders to shadow me throughout the game. There is film of me being collared around my neck, thrown to the ground, hacked at and taking cleats directly to the knees at full speed. My goodness, there were games I played with Santos in which, if today's standards of refereeing were applied, the opposing team would have had only five or six players left on the field—the others would have all received red cards!

Fair enough—that's the way the sport was played back then. It was a different, more physical game, in part because there was no TV. Nowadays, they've got high-definition cameras watching every corner of the field at all times. If the referees miss a foul, both the referees and players know they'll get an earful about it later. They'll get punished or banned retroactively, and maybe even suffer lasting damage to their reputations. Back then, however, only we and God could see most of the sins on the field. Some defenders had an awful lot of confessing to do on Sundays!

I hardly ever took this personally. After all, my defenders were usually just following orders from their coaches, and trying to earn a living for their families. Dondinho had always told me to respect my opponents. This certainly didn't stop me from throwing an elbow every now and then to defend myself. But I complained as little as possible and almost always played cleanly—in twenty years of professional soccer, I was never ejected from a game for dirty play or a hard foul. But everything in sports is a question of degrees—not even the toughest player can survive without some protection from the officials, especially if he or she is in the business of scoring goals. And in 1966, it was as if the referees had swallowed their whistles.

In that first game, against Bulgaria, we might as well have been playing in a dark alley back in Baurú, with knives and clubs and not a referee (or even a concerned parent) in sight. The Bulgarians came prepared for violence. The defender assigned to me spent the entire game kicking hard at my feet and ankles, and tripping me right in front of the referee.

"Hey! You big oaf!" I'd scream back at the defender. "This is ridiculous!" But he didn't understand a word of Portuguese, of course, and unfortunately I'd failed to brush up on my Bulgarian vulgarities. So he would just frown wordlessly back at me, and the referee always seemed to be looking the other way.

In the end, some of the fouls were so obvious that the referee had no choice but to call them. I scored on a free kick following one such foul in the first half, and Garrincha did the same in the second half. We walked away with a hard-fought 2–0 win.

It didn't feel like a victory, though. The headline the next day back home in Brazil was not the final score, but: A Hunted Pelé Leaves the Field Limping. All our other opponents now knew exactly what they could get away with. A pattern had been set. And it was, sadly, the last game Garrincha and I would ever play together.

4

I was beaten and battered, and in obvious pain, after the Bulgaria game. My right knee was killing me. But I was still preparing hard for our next match, determined not to miss any games like I had in 1958 or 1962. So I was shocked when one of the team managers informed me that I was going to sit out against Hungary.

"We want you to rest, Pelé," he told me. "We'd rather sit you now, protect you from all this rough play, and have you at full health for a game that matters."

A game that *matters*? What about the Marvelous Magyars, the team that had eliminated Brazil in 1954 and made it to the quarterfinals in 1962 as well? If we didn't win that game, there wouldn't *be* any games that mattered!

I was outraged. But, again, the pronouncements of team officials were treated as the final word. And I didn't want to create the impression that I thought I was different from anybody else. I didn't want to look like a prima donna. So I bit my tongue.

Hungary destroyed us, 3–1. The result shocked the world—it was the first World Cup game Brazil had lost since 1954 in Switzerland, also versus the Hungarians. I watched from the bench, helpless and heartbroken.

Our defeat sent the Brazilian team officials into a frenzy. Once again, just as in 1950, all of our hubris was abruptly turned on its head, and transformed into an all-consuming panic. To advance out of the round of group play, we would likely have to defeat our final opponent, Portugal, by a margin of several goals. The team managers put me back on the field, but Garrincha, Gylmar, and Djalma Santos were all relegated to the bench. Orlando, who played on our 1958 squad but hadn't played in a single World Cup match since then, was now in. All told, there were seven changes from the previous game. It was crazy, but once again—are you seeing a pattern yet?—we all kept quiet.

Once the Portugal game started, I was kicked into oblivion by their defenders, who openly targeted my lame right knee. On one play, a defender tripped me. As I was stumbling to the ground, he came at me again, feetfirst, cutting me down completely. Everybody in the entire stadium stood up screaming for a foul. Dr. Gosling and Mário Américo, the same duo who had healed my knee with the hot towels in Sweden in 1958, came sprinting out on the field. But this time there would be no miracles. I had torn a ligament in my knee.

Dr. Gosling and Mário Américo carried me off the field, with my arms draped over their shoulders and my legs suspended in the air. I couldn't put any weight at all on my right leg. But the rules of World Cup soccer at that time prohibited any substitutions or replacements, even if a player got hurt. I didn't want Brazil to be down a man in such a critical match. So after a few minutes, I went back on the field. I limped around, totally ineffective, practically hopping on one leg for the rest of the game.

Brazil lost—a 3–1 result once again, eliminating us from the World Cup.

In the end, it wouldn't be us who collected the trophy from Queen Elizabeth—but the English themselves, led by the heroics of Bobby Moore and their coach, Sir Alf Ramsey. I thought England's triumph was well deserved, and befitting the birthplace of modern soccer. Unfortunately, I never would get my chance to play at Wembley, not even in a friendly game. That omission remains one of the few true regrets of my career.

As I hopped around the field against Portugal, staggering and limping like a wounded animal, I became angrier and angrier. I was mad at the hubris of our coaches and officials. I was upset with the way Brazilian politics had intruded upon our preparations. I was furious at the referees for not protecting us. Above all, I was disappointed with myself. I was almost *always* healthy when playing for Santos, but I had now been badly injured during all three World Cups in which I'd participated. This couldn't be a coincidence, I thought. And after that game, I called the reporters over and announced my decision to never participate in another World Cup.

On our way home to Brazil from London, our flight was delayed by several hours. As with everything else during that 1966 World Cup, the team officials gave us no explanation as to why—they expected us to just sit there, docile and unquestioning. We arrived in Rio long after midnight. Those of us based in or near São Paulo were rushed directly into a waiting airplane. Only later did we discover the reason for the delays: The team officials were afraid we would be lynched by angry mobs upon our return. Their fears were unfounded—hardly anybody showed up. But the whole episode did reinforce the choice I had made. World Cup soccer seemed like something I could definitely live without.

5

"Thank God you're OK, Dico!" Mom exclaimed, near tears, when I got back home to Santos. "My knees hurt from praying for you so much!"

The 1966 World Cup was available on television in some parts of the world—but the Nascimento family wanted no part of it. No way. In the decade that I'd been playing professional soccer, Dona Celeste had never attended one of my games in person, much less watched one on TV. Most of the time, Dad couldn't stand to see the games either—I think that, for different reasons, it was too emotional for both of them. On almost every game day, with the dedication of the most devoted pilgrim, Mom would go to church and spend the duration of the match praying that I wouldn't get hurt like Dondinho had. Over the years, I think she suffered more damage to her knees than I did!

Mom and Dad weren't the only ones who suffered. In fact, everybody back home seemed to support my decision to retire from international play, including the newest member of our family: Rosemeri Cholbi, my bride.

I'd met Rose many years before—right after the 1958 Cup, in fact.

Santos was playing Corinthians, one of our biggest rivals. Brazilian teams usually put their players in a kind of quarantine the night before games—it's called a *concentração* in Portuguese, literally a "concentration"—and the goal is to isolate players from any distractions, such as . . . well, such as members of the fairer sex. But that's easier said than done, especially when Brazilian soccer players are involved, and a group of us staged a jailbreak that night. We sneaked down to the Santos gym to watch a local women's basketball match. A few of the team's players came over to talk to us, and I was surprised when one of them plopped down right next to me.

"Hi," she said. "You're Pelé, right?"

"That's right," I said, thrilled that she had recognized me.

"Don't beat Corinthians too badly tomorrow."

And with a curt smile, she walked away, returning to her team's bench.

It was the shortest of exchanges, but I was immediately smitten. She had this gorgeous, long, flowing brown hair, and—most intriguingly of all—she seemed to possess a confidence and poise that I hadn't really seen around Santos before. The next afternoon, when our game began, I found myself scanning the stands looking for this girl, when I really should have been paying attention to the action on the field. I don't remember whether we won or not, but the day still ended in disappointment—Rose wasn't there.

A few days later, I was walking down the street in Santos and happened to spot the same group of basketball players. My heart leapt. Rose wasn't with them, but the girls—giggling the whole time, of course—did tell me her name, the record store where she worked, and her age: fourteen. That was pretty young, but I was seventeen myself at the time, so it didn't seem like a deal breaker. After donning my only good pressed shirt and a nice pair of long pants, I strolled into the record store as nonchalantly as a teenage boy possibly can.

"Hello again," I said.

"Hi."

"Do you remember me?"

She nodded, smiling, seeming a bit more shy than the first time.

"Tell me," I said, "why did you want Corinthians to win if you're from Santos?"

"Because I support Corinthians," she replied. "Except I don't really like soccer."

I don't really like soccer. You might think these words would have sent me, of all people, running right out of the store! But precisely the opposite happened. I went into an even deeper swoon. At that moment, in the wake of my Swedish adventures, Rose seemed like the one person on the planet who wasn't impressed by what I had done on the field. She was clearly interested in Edson, not in Pelé.

Years passed, and I fell in love with Rose. No matter how many thousands of miles away I traveled, no matter whether we won or lost, I'd come back and there she was at home with her parents in Santos—like a rock, never changing. Our courtship was a drawn-out, very traditional affair. Rose insisted that I meet her parents right away, and they expressed their wishes that we keep things as private as possible. This was difficult—Santos was a small city, and I was who I was. But Rose never came to my games, which was hardly a sacrifice for her. When we'd go out to see a movie, Rose's aunt would come with us. The two of them would go into the cinema first. Once the lights had gone down, I'd quietly slip in and sit next to her. Our deceptions worked—nobody ever noticed that Pelé was sitting in the same theater.

Rose refused to marry me for the longest time—she was too young, she said. But in the months prior to the 1966 Cup, she finally gave in. We'd been seeing each other for more than seven years by that point. I was a two-time world champion with Brazil, Santos had won several titles, I had begun to make some real money . . . and she just didn't care. She still didn't like soccer, and she still didn't want public attention. Our engagement eventually became public, of course, and there was all kinds of buzz about where the "king of soccer" would get married. Some people suggested the Maracanã Stadium in Rio! One report said the Pope himself would officiate the ceremony. But true to form, and Rose's wishes, we held our nuptials in a house that I had bought for my parents in Santos. The ceremony was simple, officiated by a local minister, and attended by our families and just a few friends.

Even when we tried to keep things simple, though, it didn't work. There were hordes of media outside, snapping photos. Still, I went outside, smiled and waved. This, as I always told Rose, was our life. And it brought us far more good than anything else.

6

The first offer came from Tetra Pak, a Swedish packaging company. In the years after the 1958 World Cup, Sweden retained a fond place in my heart—and I always felt very welcome when Santos or the Brazilian team played friendly games in Swedish cities. But I was still a bit surprised in 1961 or so when Santos team officials first came to me and said Tetra Pak wanted me to "endorse" their product.

I telephoned Dondinho right away.

"What do you think, Dad?"

"I don't understand," he said, sounding very concerned. "You've already got a salary."

"Yes, but this would be in addition to that," I explained.

"What is it they want you to do?"

"They'll pay me to say I like their product."

This blew Dondinho's mind. "I don't know," he said. "You're an athlete, not an actor. Are they really going to pay you for *that*?"

It didn't make much sense to me either. At least not at first. American athletes had been endorsing products since at least the days of Babe Ruth, but in Brazil—as in much of the rest of the world—the concept was still quite new. Only the afterglow of that first World Cup championship made such a thing possible. I suppose people wanted to share in the feeling of being a champion, and buying products I liked was a way for them to do that. I was blessed with my mother's smile, as well. Surely that was just as important.

Still, I had some doubts. I worried that, if something I endorsed wasn't very good, people would be upset with me personally. This actually happened on a couple of occasions in the early days—I'd have people approach me on the street in Santos and complain that a product hadn't worked right. I'd always apologize profusely, and try to follow up with the company.

Despite such misgivings, we accepted the Tetra Pak offer. It would prove to be one of the best and longest-lasting relationships I ever had. That opened the floodgates: Seemingly overnight, I had so many offers from companies, both Brazilian and foreign, that I didn't know what to do with them all. I ended up hiring people just to deal with the endorsements and other business offers. One of them was my brother Zoca, who had played a few years for Santos' reserve team before deciding that soccer wasn't really his thing. He had always been superior to me in academics, and he went to law school, and became one of my most trusted advisers.

Over the years, my name and face would appear on pharmacies, gas stations, soda commercials and new apartment buildings. I endorsed a candy bar, clothing and even, if you can believe it, cattle. Some of the most energetic promotions I did were for the Brazilian coffee growers' association. Brazil was (and is) the world's biggest producer of coffee, but it had never been marketed abroad as a high-quality product. By the 1960s, our neighbors were coming up with snappy campaigns of their own, and Brazil felt pressure to match them. So when Santos played in Europe or the United States, I'd go running onto the field carrying a gigantic bag of Brazilian coffee on my back. The standard weight for coffee bags was sixty kilograms, or about 132 pounds. This was an era when I probably weighed 140 pounds wet! But hey—anything for my country, I suppose. Colombia had Juan Valdéz, and Brazil had Pelé.

One reason we had so many opportunities: Companies were starting to look to the world for business in a way they never had before. Consider the Tetra Pak example: Here was a Swedish company, hoping to profit from sales in Brazil and several other "emerging" markets. A few years before, this would have been unthinkable, but better communications and falling barriers of all kinds were making business truly global for the first time. In the 1960s, we even did a promotion for sodas in Czechoslovakia—a country that was supposedly behind the "Iron Curtain," and thus shielded from "evil" capitalism. Because my face and name were so recognizable, and I came of age just as this phenomenon was taking hold, I was often used as the tip of the sword in businesses' efforts to open up new markets. Some people have said that I was, in some respects, the first modern global icon. That sounds a bit boastful for my taste—I prefer to believe that I benefited from many global trends and coincidences. Had I been born twenty or even ten years earlier, I would have still been a good player, but the story would look quite different. I guess I was truly in the right place at the right time.

It's pretty funny to go back and see some of the ads I was in. We created a "Pelé Coffee" that is still around and quite popular in some countries even today. One TV spot shows a very elegant woman on a jet airplane—the height of glamour in the late 1960s, believe it or not—asking a stewardess: "What coffee is this?"

"It's Pelé Coffee," the stewardess answers.

"Well, it's delicious!"

Then the camera zooms in dramatically on me. I'm looking over my shoulder with my best debonair smile and a cup of steaming coffee in my hand. *Já viu, né?* I say, practically growling. Loosely translated: "You dig?"

Oh, it's impossible not to laugh at all this now! But the ads do show how long I've been around, and how much the world has changed. Ads like that didn't make much sense in 1960, and they certainly don't make much sense in 2014. Somewhere in the middle, they did. Nowadays, in our more cynical times, many ad campaigns rely on humor or irony to promote their brands. This, to be honest, has always posed a challenge. Say what you want about me, but I've always been a sincere guy.

There were lots of proposals I said no to. For years, Brazilian companies tried to get me to endorse a so-called "Pelé Pinga"—slang for cachaça, the Brazilian sugar cane alcohol used to make caipirinhas and other drinks. They wanted to make Pelé cigarettes as well. I turned those offers down, mostly because as a player I didn't consume alcohol and tobacco. I believed I needed to protect the talents that God gave me.

I always treasured the wonderful people I met through my sponsorships, and I was grateful to the companies for putting their faith in me. I was aware that every deal I did put me more squarely in the public eye—which, in turn, eroded my family's privacy. The sponsorships and business deals also meant a little less time to focus on my true love, soccer. But it was difficult to turn down some of the offers, especially for someone who came from the world that I did. My family's story showed that a soccer player's career can end with a snap of a ligament; I thought it was important to earn what I could while I could, and do things like buy my parents a nice new house in Santos—which would never have been possible without the money from sponsorships. As late as the 1960s, I wasn't even the highest-paid player on the Santos team.

Besides, I reasoned at the time, all I had to do was turn my business affairs over to my friends and associates, and they'd take care of that aspect of being Pelé. That way, I could focus primarily on soccer, and not have to worry about money.

That was another painful lesson that I would have to learn the hard way.

7

B it by bit, the wounds from 1966 began to heal. Two years after Liverpool, I finally got to put one of my biggest regrets to rest when I had the great honor of meeting Queen Elizabeth. I had always admired her quiet grace, the dignity she carried herself with and her warm smile. The queen was on a tour of South America and the world, and very graciously communicated her desire to meet me after she attended a game at the Maracanã between two all-star teams from São Paulo and Rio.

Prior to our meeting, I was paid a visit by a pair of very high-strung protocol officials from Itamaraty, the Brazilian foreign ministry. They were apparently worried their famous soccer player would go native in the presence of high royalty, and commit some sort of horrible gaffe. They gave me specific instructions on how to bow, how to listen respectfully, how not to interrupt, how to stand up straight, how to show deference . . . basically, how to drain every last ounce of humanity from our encounter.

As I took the field for the game, a huge marching band came into the Maracanã and played "God Save the Queen." I began to wonder if maybe all the formality wasn't just a figment of my handlers' imagination after all. But when the game ended and I was whisked away to a more private area to see her, all my concerns melted away. Queen Elizabeth entered the room with a huge smile, and a very informal air about her. "Mr. Pelé!" she enthused. "It's a pleasure to meet you!"

My English was still pretty awful at that point, but I'd carefully practiced a few key phrases. "Thank you very much, Your Majesty," I replied.

Everyone around us chuckled at this effort, looking quite pleased—even the guy from the foreign ministry. From that point on, we relied on the translators, but our conversation stayed very relaxed and pleasant. I said how much I had loved my time in Britain, and she talked about how her husband, Prince Philip, was a great admirer of mine. In fact, the queen herself was a much bigger soccer fan than I expected—she expressed regret that Brazil had not done better at the 1966 Cup, although she said she was very proud of the English team, of course. By the time we finished speaking, I was utterly charmed, and felt like I'd known her for ages.

I think that was the last time I ever allowed anyone to give me instructions on how to speak to someone. It was a valuable lesson: People are the same everywhere, and we need to avoid creating barriers where there are none.

In fact, the only possible breach of protocol on that day in Rio was when a member of the British delegation, maybe a diplomat, sidled up next to me and asked, in broken Portuguese, almost inaudibly, from the corner of his mouth:

"So, Pelé . . . is it *really* true you're not going to play in 1970?"

8

Out there in the world, beyond the realm of protocol officers, things were getting a lot more crazy. Throughout much of the 1960s, Santos was considered by many to be the best club team in the world. The world, meanwhile, was eager to see us play our carefree, daring, improvisational brand of soccer. We toured so often, and had so much fun while playing, that one U.S. newspaper called us "the Harlem Globetrotters of soccer." The energy and passion generated by soccer was enough to make things interesting on their own. But this was a young world, a rebellious and anarchic world, and the frenzy that constantly enveloped us—exciting, flattering and occasionally somewhat scary—seems almost inconceivable to me today.

One morning in Caracas, Venezuela, the runway was so mobbed with Santos fans that we had to wait for four hours inside our plane before police could finally clear a way out. On a trip to Egypt, we had a layover in Beirut, where an enormous crowd stormed the airport and threatened to kidnap me unless we agreed to play a match against a Lebanese team. (We politely declined, with the support of the Lebanese police, and flew on to Cairo as planned.) In Milan, Italy, a crowd of thousands caught wind that I was out shopping and tried to hunt me down for autographs. I hid behind a stone pillar, waiting for a team car to come and pick me up. When it appeared, I went sprinting into the vehicle, running faster than I ever did on a soccer field!

Even the field itself didn't offer that much protection. In 1962, we played in the finals of the Libertadores Cup—the Latin American championship, which Santos had never won before. Our opponent was Peñarol—a great team from Uruguay, which made our hearts beat even faster. After the usual home-and-away series ended in a tie, we played one final game, for all the marbles, at the Monumental Stadium in Buenos Aires, Argentina. When we won the game in rollicking fashion, by a score of 3–0 with two goals of my own, the crowd stormed the field. In the hunt for souvenirs, the fans removed literally every piece of clothing from my body! The next day, a newspaper back home featured the headline: A STRIP-TEASE, BY THE BLACK KING OF FOOTBALL.

It may sound strange, but incidents like these rarely scared anybody, especially in Latin America—a certain disorder was just part of the local landscape during those years, like rain or sunshine or smog. Each display of exuberance made Santos' legend grow. Our team featured many excellent players, including Zito, Pepe, Coutinho, and many others. Between 1958 and 1973, Santos won two Libertadores Cups, six first-division Brazilian League championships, and ten editions of the São Paulo state championship. As a result of both our success and our flair, the demand to see Santos play was insatiable. During the early part of the year, we'd tour other countries in Latin America—places like Argentina, which was much richer than Brazil back then and could afford to pay big fees. From June to August, that was Santos' big payday, when we'd travel to Europe during the northern-hemisphere summer. We'd play twenty, twenty-five or thirty games in one go.

We played everywhere: in the world's capitals, like Paris and New York, and in less-traveled destinations like Kansas City, Missouri, Alexandria, Egypt and Turin, Italy. In the Ivory Coast, in Africa, fifteen thousand people lined the road from the airport to the town center when I went to play a game in their capital, Abidjan. One time, I drove in an open car down the Champs-Élysées in Paris on our way to a match against France. The French film star Brigitte Bardot showed up at the stadium, wearing the tricolor of France—red boots, white "hot pants," and a tight-fitting blue sweater. Everybody in the stadium promptly forgot about me and the game, and spent most of the time watching her. The French team won. After the game, Bardot awarded the French captain with both the Cup and a kiss—he was so dazed afterward that the newspapers reported he left the Cup behind! Brigitte offered me a kiss, too—though I turned it down, figuring Rose wouldn't care to see pictures of that splashed across every sports page in Brazil.

The attention from fans was flattering—and relentless. On one flight from Mexico City to New York, I just leaned back and went to sleep. This is one thing I have always been able to do: close my eyes and take a nap, even if the world is collapsing around me. While I was asleep, passengers kept filing up to the front of the airplane, seeking an autograph. (This was the 1960s, when you could still get up and walk around on a plane without causing a panic.) Nobody woke me up, thankfully. As our plane started its descent into New York, a chant broke out. The passengers started serenading me in Spanish: *"Despierta, Pelé, despiertaaaaaa!"* Wake up Pelé, wake up! This stirred me, very slowly, from my slumber. I blinked open my eyes and saw the person in the seat next to me—Orlando Duarte. It took me a few minutes to realize what was going on.

"My God," I finally said to Orlando. "I thought I had died!"

We both started laughing. Once we landed, I signed autographs for everybody.

I always tried to put on a good show, because I knew I was a big reason why people came to our games. Santos would sometimes get one hundred thousand dollars for games I appeared in, and thirty thousand for games that I didn't. I appreciated that people were spending their hard-earned money to see me. All told, I scored one hundred twenty-seven goals in 1959, and one hundred ten in 1961—numbers that didn't quite seem real at the time, and seem downright impossible today. Beyond scoring, I also tried to accommodate the special requests of both the team and our hosts, some of which could be very strange. On a couple of occasions, especially in countries where black people were a less common sight, the organizers would ask either me or Coutinho to put on a white armband. They did this because, otherwise, the fans wouldn't be able to tell us apart. I guess such requests seem a bit obnoxious in today's context, but I was having too much fun to really care.

Even the little "crises" we experienced from time to time almost always had good endings. In July 1968, we were playing a game in Colombia when my teammates and I started arguing with the referee, Guillermo "Chato" Velasquez, because we thought he should have disallowed a goal scored against us. One of my teammates, Lima, went to protest his decision. The referee was a big guy—a former boxer, actually—and started to get in Lima's face—and then he sent Lima off. I was outraged, so I walked over and continued to argue—and then Chato promptly ejected me from the game, too.

I probably deserved to be sent off. But as I left the field, the Colombian crowd started going absolutely crazy. People in the stands started to throw cushions, papers and trash onto the field, at the referee, and at one another. "Pelé! Pelé!" they shouted. Police came out of the bleachers to protect Chato.

I ran into the dressing room under the bleachers, but the noise from the crowd remained just as deafening. There was stomping, firecrackers and this high-pitched roar. It pretty much sounded like World War III out there.

I had begun to take off my shoes when the director of Santos came running in, short of breath.

"You're coming back into the game," he said.

"What?" I replied, incredulous. "Are you crazy? I was sent off."

"No, no," he said, shaking his head. "The referee has been removed from the game, and you're coming back."

I couldn't believe it—but the director really was telling the truth! With the entire stadium in revolt, the authorities decided that putting me back into the game was the only way to avoid a full-fledged riot. So I put my shoes back on and ran back out there. We continued the game, with Chato nowhere to be seen.

The incident was pretty funny, but it also felt wrong. Chato was the

At the North American Soccer League playoffs in 1977. / En los playoffs de la Liga Norteamericana de Fútbol en 1977.

José Dias Herrera

During the early days of my career with Santos Football Club. /
Durante los primeros días de mi carrera con el Santos Futebol Clube.

Popperfoto/Getty Images

Eyes on the ultimate prize: the Jules Rimet World Cup trophy, circa
1958. / Con los ojos en el premio más importante: el trofeo Jules
Rimet de la Copa del Mundo, alrededor de 1958.

I had the opportunity to meet King Gustaf VI Adolf of Sweden before the final match of the World Cup against Sweden in 1958. Brazil won 5 to 2. / Tuve la oportunidad de conocer al rey Gustavo VI Adolfo de Suecia antes del partido final de la Copa del Mundo en 1958. Brasil le ganó a Suecia 5 a 2.

Playing soccer gave me the opportunity to see the world. / Jugar fútbol me dio la oportunidad de conocer el mundo.

A beautiful moment. Celebrating Brazil's World Cup victory over Italy in Mexico City, 1970. / Un momento hermoso. Celebrando la victoria de Brasil sobre Italia en la Copa Mundial en la Ciudad de México, 1970.

Meeting Robert Kennedy in 1965. I was proud to work with Eunice Kennedy Shriver on promoting the Special Olympics, which she founded. / Con Robert Kennedy en 1965. Me sentí orgulloso de trabajar con Eunice Kennedy Shriver, promocionando los Juegos Olímpicos especiales, que ella fundó.

Hulton Archive/Getty Images

AP Photo

While on an official visit of South America in 1968, Queen Elizabeth II and her husband, Prince Philip, greeted me after a local game in Rio de Janeiro. / Durante una visita oficial a Suramérica en 1968, la reina Isabel II y su esposo el príncipe Felipe me saludaron después de un partido en Río de Janeiro.

AP Photo

Visiting Paris in 1971, where I played an exhibition match with Santos FC to benefit cancer research. / Visitando París en 1971, donde jugué en un partido de exhibición con el Santos Futebol Clube en beneficio de la investigación del cáncer.

José Dias Herrera

Taking in the sights while in Europe. / De turismo en Europa.

President Richard Nixon invited me to the White House in 1973. / El presidente Richard Nixon me invitó a la Casa Blanca en 1973.

With President Gerald Ford, 1974. / Con el presidente Gerald Ford, 1974.

When I came to America, I learned about this "other" game of football. I remember Joe Namath (of the Jets) asking if I ever thought of kicking field goals in the NFL. My answer to him: "I cannot score any goals with a helmet on!" / Cuando vine a Estados Unidos, me enteré de esta «otra» forma del fútbol. Recuerdo que Joe Namath (de los Jets) me preguntó si yo había considerado patear goles de campo en la NFL. Le respondí: «¡No puedo marcar un solo gol con un casco!».

With President Jimmy Carter, 1977. / Con el presidente Jimmy Carter, 1977.

Playing for the New York Cosmos, 1977. / Jugando con el Cosmos de Nueva York, 1977.

The New York Cosmos

Playing with the New York Cosmos gave me the opportunity to popularize the beautiful game in the U.S. / Jugar con el Cosmos de Nueva York me dio la oportunidad de popularizar el «juego bonito» en Estados Unidos.

The final game of my career, New York Cosmos versus Santos Football Club, 1977. I shouted "Love! Love! Love!" to the crowd and asked everyone to pay attention to the children of the world. / El último partido de mi carrera: los Cosmos de Nueva York contra el Santos Futebol Clube, 1977. Grité «¡Amor! ¡Amor! ¡Amor!» a la multitud y pedí a todos que prestaran atención a los niños del mundo.

My friend and confidant Julio Mazzei played a huge role in persuading me to come to the United States. / Mi amigo y confidente Julio Mazzei fue decisivo en persuadirme para ir a jugar en Estados Unidos.

My friend Muhammad Ali and me before the final game of my career at the Giants Stadium on October 1, 1977. I played one half for the New York Cosmos and the other half for Santos. Cosmos won 2-1. / Mi amigo Muhammad Alí y yo antes del último partido de mi carrera en el Giants Stadium el 1 de octubre de 1977. Jugué el primer tiempo con el Cosmos de Nueva York, y el segundo con el Santos. El Cosmos ganó 2-1.

With President Ronald Reagan, I am showing ball control to a children's soccer team at the White House in 1982. / Con el presidente Ronald Reagan, enseñando en la Casa Blanca a un equipo infantil de fútbol cómo controlar el balón, en 1982.

With Vice President Al Gore in Los Angeles at the 1994 World Cup. / Con el vicepresidente Al Gore en Los Ángeles durante la Copa Mundial de 1994.

During a 1997 trip to Rio de Janeiro, President Clinton visited the Mangueira School, which teaches impoverished children how to build strong bodies and minds. / Durante un viaje a Río de Janeiro en 1997 el presidente Clinton visitó la Escuela Mangueira, y enseñó a los niños pobres a desarrollar cuerpos y mentes fuertes.

With Brazil president Dilma Rousseff and FIFA president Sepp Blatter during the preliminary draw of the 2014 World Cup in Rio de Janeiro, 2011. / Con la presidenta de Brasil Dilma Rousseff y el presidente de la FIFA «Sepp» Blatter durante el sorteo preliminar de la Copa Mundial de 2014 en Río de Janeiro, 2011.

Kicking around the ball with President Clinton in Rio de Janeiro. / Pateando el balón con el presidente Clinton en Río de Janeiro.

With longtime friend Henry Kissinger during the closing ceremony of the 2012 London Olympic Games. / Con mi gran amigo Henry Kissinger durante la ceremonia de clausura de los Juegos Olímpicos de Londres en 2012.

John Stillwell/AFP/Getty Images

The Yomiuri Shimbun via AP Images

Visiting Japan in 2011 and commemorating the lives lost in the devastating earthquake and tsunami that struck the country earlier that year. / Visitando Japón en 2011, en conmemoración de las vidas perdidas tras el devastador terremoto y tsunami que azotaron al país a comienzos de ese año.

At the 2013 New York Cosmos Legends Gala being honored by HELP USA. / En la Gala de Leyendas del Cosmos de Nueva York, siendo homenajeado por HELP USA.

In 2012, outside 10 Downing Street in London with British Prime Minister David Cameron. / En 2012, afuera del 10 Downing Street —residencia oficial del primer ministro— en Londres, con el primer ministro británico David Cameron.

Joshua Ponte

Kicking the ball around with children during the 2012 African Cup of Nations in Gabon. / Pateando el balón con unos niños durante la Copa Africana de Naciones en Gabón, en 2012.

referee, and he made a decision to throw me out. His decision should have been respected. For years afterward, I felt bad whenever I thought of what happened that day. Luckily, in the long run, I was able to make some amends. The healing process started when I saw Chato in a hotel in Brazil. We hugged, and exchanged contact information. When I played in New York near the end of my career, I sent him and his family tickets to one of our games. Finally, in Miami, during one of my farewell games near the end of my career, some journalists decided that we should do a "reenactment" of the expulsion. Chato pulled a red card out to send me off the field once again. I snatched the card from his hand and then kept right on playing, just as I had in Colombia!

We all had a good laugh about it—especially Chato. What could have been a lifelong grudge ended in a friendship. That's another great thing about soccer—most of the time, everybody walks away happy.

9

As fun as it all was, something in my life was missing. And people kept reminding me of it, again and again.

"Don't you miss playing for your country?" they'd ask. "Do you want 1966 to be the last memory people have of you in a Brazilian uniform?" Fans, Santos team officials, Brazilians on the street, journalists, other players—always the same questions, and I never had a convincing answer. Oh sure, I'd say something about having played in three World Cups, and having been injured in all of them, and how the referees hadn't protected me, and so on. But whenever I said these things, they seemed out of character, like I was playing another role. They didn't seem like things Pelé would say.

A few years before, in 1964, Santos hired a new technical director: Professor Júlio Mazzei. He quickly became one of the most important people in my life. A tremendously educated man who had studied in the United States, Professor Mazzei basically took over all aspects of the team's physical preparation. Apart from our training, he also acted like a kind of counselor—helping all the players learn how to behave properly in hotels, in airports, and in other places when we were on the road. He was kind of a bridge that took us from the world of amateur athletics to the growing pressures of professional sports in the 1960s and 1970s; he helped all of us boys start to become men. Over the years, Professor Mazzei would be a constant source of stability and perspective; he was often the only person who could see people and events with a certain distance in my crazy life, and I trusted him immensely. He was like the older brother I never had.

One thing I loved about Professor Mazzei was that he talked to me like nobody else could. He never pushed that hard, and he always used good humor. But he was always very honest, while trying to nudge me in the right direction. So around that time, I'd be working out or doing drills on the field, and he'd say:

"Ahhhh, Pelé, looking good. You're ready to win a third Cup for Brazil!"

I'd just smile at him and mutter something under my breath.

"What are you going to say when 1970 comes around and you're just sitting at home?" he'd continue, laughing. "What are you going to tell your family?"

"They were the ones who wanted me to quit!" I'd protest. "The answer is still no, Professor!"

Professor Mazzei would throw up his hands in mock despair and walk away.

What was really going on?

Well, by the time I reached my late twenties, I think that in certain situations I'd become a pretty stubborn guy. I'd been in the spotlight for nearly a decade, and burned more than once in soccer, in business, and in life. I had learned the hard way that, when it came to my career, in particular, it was important to say "no" more often than I said "yes." Once I said no, I rarely changed my mind. Was that the greatest way to live one's life? No, but it helped protect me. It gave me a bit of peace.

In truth, I *did* deeply miss playing for the Brazilian national team. But I also believed that, before I could come back, something needed to change.

That something was me.

The first World Cup championship, in Sweden, had been a magical ride, no doubt. The image of me as the boyish teenage phenom, carried by sheer talent to heights few had reached before in soccer, had endured. In the years since, I had continued to thrive as a guy who just loved the game, and loved scoring goals. But in more recent years, there had been talk that, for all of my ability on the field, I was a solitary, even aloof figure off of it. For example, after we got bounced out of the 1966 World Cup in England, the *Sunday Times* of London said the image of me leaving the field hurt reinforced the image of Pelé as "the sad millionaire . . . an introverted, remote figure imprisoned in the shell that protects him from the crushing weight of his fame."

Some of these portrayals of me as a lonely superstar were utter nonsense, invented by journalists and others to create controversy and sell newspapers. For example, there was speculation in the press, going all the way back to the early 1960s, that Garrincha and I didn't get along. Most of these were based on the theory that he and I had fallen out over a woman: Elza Soares, a famous Brazilian samba singer.

The truth was actually pretty funny. After I hurt my groin at the 1962 World Cup, I did all kinds of rehab in a desperate effort to get back on the field. One afternoon, while still in Chile, I was sitting half-naked on a training table when who should walk in but Elza. She looked gorgeous, as always—sultry, poised, full of life. I have no idea how she managed to get into our dressing room though! Surprised, I grabbed a towel, and once I was covered up, I began chatting easily with her. While we were talking, Garrincha came into the room and joined us. I could tell right away that Garrincha was bewitched, and even after Elsa left, he still seemed to be lost in a daze.

"Man, Pelé," he said quietly. "Man, that girl Elza is really cool."

"Yup," I agreed.

"Man, she's just marvelous. Wow. What a girl."

I sat there, silently, a smile spreading across my face.

"Man, if . . ." And then Garrincha stopped himself. "Well," he said, "it's too bad that I'm married!"

In the end, that didn't stop him. Garrincha and Elza started seeing each other during that World Cup—which, of course, also saw Garrincha give one of the greatest individual performances in soccer history, leading us to the 1962 championship even after all the rehab failed to put me back on the field. Garrincha eventually left his wife to be with Elza, and they got married. This led to whispers that he had "stolen" her from me, and that I hated him for it. That obviously wasn't true!

In reality, I loved Garrincha. I loved his playful spirit. I loved that, even after he won the world championship twice, he was still the guy who would run around the Brazilian team bus, throwing ice water in people's faces to wake them up. I was always grateful to him for running over to help me when I passed out on that field in Sweden. We shared the bond of having been underestimated because of our humble roots—the two country hicks who were most scrutinized by the team doctors in 1958. Right after my injury in 1962, Garrincha kept assuring me that I'd be back on the field in no time. "You're not going to abandon me, are you?" he'd say good-naturedly. He also said that, if all else failed, he'd suggest to the team medics that they send me to his hometown, Pau Grande, to see a faith healer—surely she would get the job done.

I got along well with Garrincha, and virtually everybody else. But as I got older, I began to see that "getting along" was not always enough. I was affable and I worked hard, yes. I always gave every effort on the field. But the first chapter of my life, when it was enough for me to just score as many goals as I could, without fulfilling any kind of greater role, had obviously come to an end.

Deep in my heart, I felt like I needed to grow up. After all, I was no longer the boy who took the field in Sweden, or even the twenty-one-year-old who had played in the 1962 Cup in Chile. I was a man now. By the 1970 Cup, I would be twenty-nine—only a year younger than Didi was when he carried our young team with his maturity and steadying presence in Sweden. I guess there comes a moment in every person's life when they realize they need to live for others, and not just for themselves. For me, this change didn't happen overnight, and it wasn't primarily the result of anything that happened on the soccer field. Rather, it was another life event—the birth of my first child, Kely Cristina, in 1967. As she started to grow up, and act more like a little person, she changed the way I looked at everyone—including my teammates. I came to deeply relish the feeling of looking after others, of helping people. I realized that if Edson was capable of this, so was Pelé.

Meanwhile, I knew that, once again, the world was changing fast. When we traveled to Sweden in 1958, Brazil took everyone by surprise. People knew practically nothing about our country, or our team. Television was a rarity, and there was little film of us playing together that our opponents might use to learn our strengths and weaknesses. This remained true well into the 1960s. In fact, several of the most memorable goals of my career were never caught on film or TV. One example was the so-called *gol de placa* or "Plaque Goal" that I scored for Santos at the Maracanã in 1961—in the absence of video, the team officials wanted to commemorate it in some way, so they put a plaque outside the stadium that explained how I weaved around defenders to score that goal. Still, only the fans who were present in the stadium that day would have any real memory of what happened.

This sounds simple, but it actually had lots of consequences on the way our team operated and prepared—and it even dictated our style of play. With no real record of our performances, we were free to play like a group of talented individuals, rather than a real team. We didn't need any sophisticated strategy—we could just rely on our instincts and have fun on the field. Brazil was especially good at this, and it was a reason we had been so successful. But now, even though we weren't even a decade removed from the Sweden Cup, the spread of television was starting to pull the curtain down on everything in the world—soccer included. We'd already seen this at the 1966 World Cup in England: Teams had prepared for us, and they were starting to employ very complex game plans. Now it wasn't enough to just get a bunch of talented guys together and motivate them. You had to have tactics, teamwork—and leadership.

In that context, I saw the errors of 1966 in a new light. That moment after the Scotland tie when the coaches berated us, and Garrincha and I just shrugged at each other in the hallway afterward—that had been a mistake. We were established, important team figures by then, and we could have spoken up for what we knew was right. Similarly, when the team decided not to play me in the ill-fated game that same year against Hungary, I could have done more than just meekly accept my fate.

Maybe it was necessary for us to lose in England for me to see all of this. Maybe it was necessary for me to step away from the international game for a period. Meanwhile, there had been other positive changes—Santos was playing well, and I was the leading scorer, which meant that my health was back to one hundred percent and I could go play for Brazil again without worrying about neglecting my club team. There was also now a more subdued, controlled atmosphere around the international game—some changes had been made following the 1966 tournament, such as allowing players who get hurt midgame, as I had, to be substituted. The 1970 Cup would also be the first to have yellow and red cards, partly to discourage the kind of brutish behavior we'd seen in England.

After considerable thought, and conversations with everybody from Professor Mazzei to Rose and Mom and Dad, I called the team leadership and asked them if they'd take me back. Thankfully, they said yes. I vowed to them, then and there, that from that moment on I would focus not only on being a good goal scorer, but a good leader as well.

10

Well, easier said than done!

In early 1969, a little more than a year before we were to leave for Mexico, the directors surprised us by bringing in a new coach: João Saldanha. Saldanha was a well-known journalist who had been one of the loudest critics of our chaotic, overconfident approach in 1966. He was a charismatic whirlwind of a man, always well-spoken and very sure of himself. Whereas the previous coaches seemed afraid to offend anyone by committing to one player or another, Saldanha declared right away that he was going to select a core group of players and stick with them.

"My team is made of eleven beasts who are ready for anything," Saldanha told his former colleagues in the press. "They'll stick with me until the end. It's glory or bust!"

Thus, we became known as "Saldanha's Beasts." And in the beginning, it seemed like a pretty good mix. Rather than trying to pick an all-star team of Brazilian players, Saldanha wanted to foster unity by putting together a core from just a few club teams. By selecting clusters of players who already knew one another, we'd solve the issues of chemistry we'd had in the past. So many of us came from Santos and Botafogo, the two best club teams of the era. We won almost all of our games in 1969, beating all six of our opponents in the qualifying round—which had never been done before.

Unfortunately, Saldanha also had a dark side. What seemed like confidence in the beginning turned into a dangerous, erratic arrogance. He was very volatile, and everybody knew that he liked to drink. *The New York Times* described him in a long profile piece as "outspoken, quick-tempered, aggressive and Quixotic." He developed a habit of berating anyone in the press, or even in the stands, who dared to question his coaching. In one notorious incident, Saldanha was so angered by criticism from a club team coach in Rio that he reportedly went after the guy with a gun. It was a miracle that nobody got hurt.

The intrigue began to take its toll on the field. At the end of the year, we lost a friendly match against Atlético Mineiro—the club team Dondinho had auditioned for back in 1942—by a 2–1 score. We lost 2–0 to Argentina at a game in Porto Alegre, in southern Brazil. Meanwhile, Saldanha traveled to Mexico and Europe to scout our future opponents. Upon his return, he started randomly cutting some players from the squad and inviting others, breaking up the core that, all things considered, was still playing pretty well.

This time, I resolved not to repeat my mistakes from 1966—I would not be the quiet superstar any longer. I had learned my lesson, and I decided to speak up. I tried first to talk directly to Saldanha, but I couldn't even get him to sit down with me. So, somewhat reluctantly, I went to the press instead. "Isn't it a little early to be making so many changes to the team?" I said. "I don't think this is the best moment for new players."

I guess I was lucky that Saldanha didn't come after me with a gun. But close enough! He began telling the press that it was time for a "new generation" of Brazilian players to get their chance. Before a game against Argentina, he left me out of the starting lineup for what he said were reasons of discipline. As another game with Chile approached, Saldanha said he was considering removing me from the team altogether, alleging that my poor eyesight—myopia—was a handicap in night games.

The myopia charge was pretty funny, actually. It's true that I'm nearsighted—I always have been, and the issue was diagnosed by the doctors at Santos when I first arrived there at age fifteen. But it never interfered with my play—in fact, it may have even helped it. One of the more interesting theories over the years for my success, put forth by some journalists, was that I had extra-peripheral vision that allowed me to see a wider swath of the field than most players. I have no idea whether this is true—but the point is, my vision certainly wasn't a problem.

Everybody knew what Saldanha was trying to do. His behavior had become unsustainable. Prior to the Chile game, the team management fired Saldanha. I stayed in the lineup and scored two of our five goals.

Was that the end of the mess? Goodness, no. Back now in the realm of journalism, with all the power and none of the responsibility he'd had before, Saldanha ripped into all of us with a renewed vengeance. He said that Gérson, one of our star midfielders, suffered from psychological problems. Leão, the reserve goalkeeper, was struggling because his arms were too short, he said. As for me, once the whole myopia story was exposed as a red herring, Saldanha changed his tune and said I was horribly out of shape. That, too, was a lie—so then he modified his story yet again. Speaking on television late one night, Saldanha said the sad truth was that Pelé had a very serious disease, but he was not at liberty to disclose what it was.

I watched all of this live, from home, as he said it. It *sounded* false, and of course I felt perfectly fine—but Saldanha seemed so thoroughly convinced that I began to wonder. Was it possible that Saldanha knew something I didn't? Could the team officials be hiding something from me, either out of pity or, more likely, the desire to have me win the 1970 Cup free of distractions? This was, after all, the same team that once had screened our mail, and forbidden us from questioning their orders. In the Brazil of that era, where soccer players were sometimes treated as property, anything was possible.

The more I thought about it, the more convinced I was that I might have some terrible disease like cancer. I couldn't sleep that night. The next morning, I went to the head of the technical commission and our team doctor and I demanded to know the truth—was I sick or not? They said the whole thing was nonsense, and just an excuse by Saldanha to save some face in the public eye. But it wasn't until I examined both my recent and past medical reports with my own eyes that I finally began to relax.

Time has passed, and so has my anger over what happened. Saldanha suffered from many problems, some of which might have been beyond his control. He does deserve some credit for laying the foundation for the 1970 team, and for helping Brazilian soccer begin to get its self-esteem back. In the end, he died doing what he loved, passing away in Italy while attending the 1990 World Cup—as a journalist.

11

Our new coach was not only the anti-Saldanha in terms of demeanor, but a former teammate and dear friend of mine—Mário Zagallo. A key player on the World Cup–winning teams of 1958 and 1962, Zagallo had always played soccer with a chip on his shoulder, for a reason I could certainly identify with. Zagallo had been on the field at the Maracanã in 1950, as an eighteen-year-old soldier taking part in the pregame festivities. He stayed and watched the match, and was one of the many Brazilians who vowed, each in his or her own way, to avenge the loss against Uruguay.

Although he was just thirty-nine when he took over as our coach, and only six years older than the senior player on the team, Zagallo in a very short time established himself as a skilled tactician who—refreshingly—refused to play mind games. He had the respect of the players for both his championship pedigree and his reputation for immense physical strength—Zagallo had grown up swimming in the rough tides of Brazil's northeast, and every single move he made conveyed authority and self-assurance. He was, in fact, the calmest man I have ever known.

Right away, I sought out Zagallo and assured him I wouldn't be any trouble—that the situation with Saldanha was unique, and wouldn't be repeated.

"If you don't want to play me, I'll understand," I said. "I won't protest, I promise. But please just tell me so directly, instead of playing games."

Zagallo just laughed. "Pelé," he said, clasping his huge hand on my shoulder, "I'm no fool. You'll be on the field, trust me."

Zagallo was self-assured enough to retain the core of the team that Saldanha put together, with only a few changes. Among them, he made the very wise decision to promote Eduardo Gonçalves de Andrade, nicknamed Tostão, or "little coin," one of the greatest talents and most vivid characters ever to play for Brazil. Tostão made his debut in the big leagues at age fifteen, and his youth and skill as an attacking forward led some people to call him the "White Pelé." Extremely intelligent on and off the field, Tostão would later become a medical doctor. There was some speculation in the press that it was impossible for the two of us to be on the field together—our styles were very similar—but Zagallo had the confidence and wisdom to dismiss those concerns. In fact, some people later observed that the 1970 team actually had four or five "number tens" on the field at any given time.

This was highly unusual, and some critics disparaged us as a team of all attackers and no defense. But Zagallo believed that he could play as many talented players as he wanted, as long as he encouraged us to work together. That sounds simple, but I had seen throughout my career how hard this concept was to execute. Zagallo encouraged all of us to speak up, to provide input, to help him make decisions. It was the opposite of the authoritarian, say-nothing climate of 1966. We had team meetings where *everybody* spoke. Zagallo would sit there and listen. He had the confidence to gather input from everyone. And thus, slowly, a real team began to be born.

12

As we got ready to leave for Mexico, politics again intruded on our preparations—in maybe the most amazing way ever.

The new chief of the military government, Emílio Médici, was a conservative, a hard-liner—and a big-time soccer fan. He followed the ups and downs of the Brazilian team for many years while rising through the army. But we were still very surprised when Médici gave a newspaper interview saying he wanted to see his favorite player, Dario José dos Santos, on the Brazilian national team at the 1970 World Cup.

Dario, known as "Dada Maravilha" or "Marvelous Dada," was in fact a very good player. He would go down as one of the most prolific goal scorers in Brazilian history. But we already had more than our share of offensive firepower on the team, and we had worked very hard to develop a core nucleus of players that knew and trusted one another. So, at that late stage, there wasn't really any room for Dario on our squad.

Why would Médici say such a thing? Perhaps because he was a true fan of Dario's, and the sport. But there were other things going on in Brazil at that time, things that were only increasing the pressure on our team to be successful at the World Cup in Mexico. The military dictatorship had taken a much more authoritarian and repressive turn in the late 1960s, and was now censoring media and purging universities and other institutions of suspected "subversives." Thousands of Brazilians were forced into exile, and the unofficial slogan of those years was Brazil: *ame-o ou deixe-o.* "Love it or leave it." Worst of all, the military stepped up its horrible practice of abducting and torturing people. During those first few months of 1970, as we were busy training and preparing for the World Cup, a twenty-two-year-old university student named Dilma Rousseff was being tortured in a jail cell in southern Brazil, hung upside down from a metal rod by her knees while electric shocks were applied to her body.

When we first started hearing such stories, we almost couldn't believe them—they sounded like things that would happen in Nazi Germany, not in our beloved Brazil. This was still a few years before the coup by Augusto Pinochet in Chile—or the notorious "Dirty War" period in Argentina—illustrated to the world just how brutal South American dictatorships could be. Soon, though, some players and members of the Brazilian coaching staff were hearing firsthand accounts of the horrors. While we still didn't know the scale of what was happening, we could no longer doubt its existence. As a team, we had long discussions among the players about what was going on. Should we say something? Should we make a protest of some kind?

We decided in the end that we were soccer players, not politicians. We didn't think it was our place to speak up about what was happening. Zagallo put Dario on the team, as requested. And we all kept quiet—at least for a while.

13

Of all the World Cups I've attended, Mexico 1970 was by far the craziest—and the most fun. There were a great many challenges, including the heat, the altitude, and the chaos that seemed to surround our team at all times. But the raucous, highly knowledgeable Mexican fans loved us—and thank God, because if we hadn't had them on our side, all might well have been lost.

To cite just one example of the fans' passion: After the Mexican team crushed El Salvador by a score of 4–0 in group play, tens of thousands of people surged into the streets of Mexico City, ignoring the pouring rain. The crowd scaled the wall in front of the hotel where the international press was staying, and knocked loose a twelve-foot-tall fiberglass soccer ball that had been manufactured just for the World Cup. Screaming and shouting with joy, the crowd rolled the giant ball down the street for two miles to the city's main square, the Zócalo. There, they happily tore their prize into shreds and handed out the pieces as delighted souvenirs.

Several teams could never quite adjust to the conditions. Some of the venues really were quite difficult—games in the host city of Toluca, for example, were played at a staggering nine thousand feet above sea level, about twice the altitude of Denver, Colorado. Some of the games started at noon, in the brutal glare of the Mexican sun, in an effort by FIFA to maximize the TV audience back in Europe. Some players simply couldn't take the heat. In a few matches, including one between Germany and Peru, some observers noticed that the teams seemed to be playing mostly in the tiny sliver of shade provided by the stadium's grandstands.

It was the first World Cup held in Latin America since Brazil in 1950, and the Europeans, in particular, were wary of what exotic ills and hazards might await them. The English brought their own bottled water from home, and even tried to import bacon and sausage, plus their own bus and card tables. But things didn't quite work out—Mexican law banned everyone, including soccer players, from importing food that might transmit hoof-and-mouth disease. All the English sausages were destroyed at the airport, and the team had to survive on spicy Mexican *salchichas* instead.

Brazil was not immune from the anything-goes atmosphere. Shortly before we arrived, Mexican authorities arrested nine people whom they said were part of a complex international plot to kidnap me. After the arrests, I was ordered by team officials to sleep in a different hotel room each night. Security at our team facilities was increased, and I had a guard assigned to me at all times. It all sounds terrifying now, and I guess in some ways it was. But at the time I didn't think about it very much. Like I've said, in those years, you had to kind of embrace the chaos. So I did. And, as usual, I slept like a baby.

Everything Zagallo and the team management did helped us to feel like we were living in a lush, quiet, drama-free oasis. Our team was the first of the sixteen competing countries to arrive, landing in Mexico about a month before our first game. Officially, our early arrival was supposed to help us adjust to the altitude in Guadalajara, where we would be playing our group matches. But I think the managers mostly just wanted to get us into one place and make us comfortable, to avoid the Carnival-like chaos of 1966. They wanted us to spend time together, to practice together, to bond.

By that point, the same core group had already been playing together for a year and a half. On the field, I sometimes knew what move my teammates would make before they did, and vice versa. Once we got to Mexico, an even deeper bond took hold off the field as well. We ate our meals together, we watched soccer on television together, and we began to feel like true brothers.

One night, I was on the phone with Rose, and she told me that the family was getting together every day to pray for us. I thought: Wouldn't it be wonderful if we gathered a prayer group on the team too? I explained the idea first to Carlos Alberto, the captain of that 1970 team and one of my teammates from Santos. He thought it was a fantastic plan. Then we talked to Antonio do Passo, one of the team managers, and we were soon joined by Tostão, Piazza, and our venerable trainer, Mário Américo. Before long, nearly all of the forty or so players and members of the delegation were gathering every night after dinner to pray together. It wasn't compulsory, of course—but almost everybody came anyway, regardless of whether they were Catholic or not.

We found something to pray for every day: the sick, the war in Vietnam, the political situation back home, the health of a loved one. We never prayed to win the World Cup. We asked only that no one get seriously injured, and that God help bring all of us close together and keep our families safe.

That 1970 team, frankly, didn't have as much talent as the squad we had assembled in Sweden in 1958. We had weaknesses that were there for everyone to see. Few people back in Brazil expected us to win the championship—some journalists didn't even think we'd make it out of group play. But, as we prayed and spent all of our days together, I saw something happening that, in more than a decade of professional soccer, I'd never quite seen before. In our practices, and then our games, our performance was even greater than the sum of our individual abilities. We began playing phenomenally well. And we realized that we really had something special on our hands.

This was the big lesson of soccer that, prior to that 1970 Cup, I hadn't fully learned. In Mexico, amid the prayer sessions, the practices, the team meetings, the meals, the jokes, the camaraderie, I finally realized the full potential of what a group of players can do together. I saw the true power of a *team*.

14

Another funny thing about the 1970 World Cup: It was like a procession of the most horrifying, disturbing ghosts from Brazil's soccer past. We'd have to confront our fears, and slay them one by one, if we wanted to be crowned champions once again.

The first game was no exception.

Our opponent was Czechoslovakia—the team against which I'd suffered my severe muscle strain in the 1962 Cup, putting me out of the rest of the tournament. Despite the trauma from my injury, I also remembered that game for one of the most outstanding demonstrations of sportsmanship I ever saw during my career. After I got hurt, and stayed on the field, the Czech players could easily have "gone in for the kill" by targeting my injury or otherwise being rough with me. That would have sent me off the field, and put their team in a better position to win. But it also could possibly have caused a longer-term or even a permanent injury to me. So instead, the Czechs opted to gently neutralize me for the rest of the game. Three players in particular—Masopust, Popluhár and Lála—would back off of me just a bit whenever the ball was passed to me. They sought to prevent me from doing anything dangerous, yes, but they also let me finish my plays. That game ended in a goalless tie. Even today, I remain very grateful to the Czechs for the gallant way they treated me.

Oddsmakers had rated the Czech team as one of the strongest in the Cup in 1970, and we weren't about to take them lightly, given how rigorously they'd played us in the past. But we had access to videotape now, and I spent considerable time watching games from Europe. In the tape, and in friendly matches we'd played, I noticed that European goalies had lately adopted a new technique—they often strayed far from their goal when the ball was on the other side of the field, almost acting like another defender. So when the game started, and I saw that the Czech goalkeeper Viktor was doing precisely that, I decided to try my luck.

I was jogging forward, about to cross the halfway line and about sixty-five yards from the opponents' goal, when I lofted the ball up into the air. Right away, I could hear people in the crowd start to murmur—"What on earth is Pelé trying to do?" But as the ball arced back down toward the earth, and bent inward toward the right goalpost, and Viktor sprinted in a panic back toward the goal, it all became clear. The crowd's murmur turned into a roar.

As I raced down the field, I could see the ball curving, curving . . . and, alas, it rolled just outside of the goalpost. No goal. The crowd groaned in disappointment, then began to applaud in appreciation of the effort. As for Viktor, he looked relieved but somewhat disturbed, like he'd just survived a horrible car accident.

Oddly enough, some people say that shot was the most memorable single moment of the 1970 Cup. In fact, even today when people meet me they say it's one of the plays from my career they remember best. It's just a shame the damn ball didn't go in the goal!

Whatever disappointment I may have felt, it didn't last long. We were tied 1–1 at halftime, but shortly after the second half began, Gérson sent me a long, high pass. I let it bounce off of my chest. Before it hit the ground—and before Viktor realized what was happening—I volleyed the ball into the net to put Brazil in front 2 to 1.

The Czechs were good sports once again that afternoon, but our team just had too much offensive firepower. Jairzinho, our star forward, added two more goals—beginning an unprecedented and remarkable streak of his own. The game's final score was Brazil 4, Czechoslovakia 1. We showed our ability to play as a team, we refused to be intimidated by our past mistakes, and with a handful of circus moves like the shot from midfield, we served notice to our opponents that the old, flamboyant Brazilian style of play was alive and well.

So much for myopia!

15

Our next game was a battle royale between the two previous World Cup champions—us against England. It was a matchup that I had yearned for four years previously, and that I was desperate to play in. We knew it would be one of the toughest games of the entire 1970 Cup. However, we also knew we had a formidable secret weapon on our side—the Mexican crowd.

The English coach, Sir Alf Ramsey, was a good man and a fine tactician whose work I always admired. Unfortunately, he had angered some people back in 1966 when he described the Argentine team as "animals" after England beat them on their way to the World Cup championship. Many Latin Americans took the comment personally, and weren't very shy about expressing their feelings. The night before our game, a crowd of around two hundred people gathered outside the England team hotel, most of them carrying drums, frying pans, horns and other noisemaking devices. They serenaded the English team until about three in the morning, when armed guards finally started firing into the air to drive them away.

Like I said, it was one crazy World Cup!

Meanwhile, Ramsey had also boldly predicted that England would not only win our group, but also go on to repeat its championship of 1966. Fair enough—he had a very good team, including Bobby Moore, Bobby Charlton and many other top-notch players from four years previous. But, on the day of our game, the fans in the Guadalajara stadium seemed to be just continuing their long blowout party from the night before—I'd never heard such a raucous crowd. The stands were filled almost entirely with Mexicans—the contingent of Brazilian fans was estimated at only about two thousand people—but almost everyone was cheering for Brazil. It felt like we were playing before a home crowd. It was absolutely marvelous.

We also knew that the world would be watching as it never had before. Television had become much more widespread in the previous four years, and the 1970 Cup was the first to have broadcasts in color. The Brazil-England game was probably, at that point, the most-watched event in world history, journalists wrote. In England alone, some twenty-nine million people watched, nearly as many as saw the first moon landing the year before.

Coach Zagallo, calm as ever, told us before the game to ignore all the hype, and not to get carried away by the pro-Brazil crowd. "Don't expect to just samba your way through this game," he warned. "And don't expect any quick goals either!"

Ten minutes in, I thought I might just prove him wrong. Jairzinho made a great move to get past his English defender and he made a perfect high cross into the penalty box. I leapt into the air and—keeping my eyes open, as always—headed the ball down just inside the post. The moment I hit it, I knew it was a goal. But the English goalkeeper, Gordon Banks, made an amazing leaping save all the way from the other post, and managed to just barely scoop the ball up and over the bar. It was one of the best saves ever in a World Cup, if not the best, and the game remained tied going into halftime.

In retrospect, I think the header might have been too individualistic a way for us to win the game. If our 1970 squad was all about teamwork, then we had to score on a true team goal—one that reflected the rapport we'd spent the past year developing.

And so, fourteen minutes into the second half, Tostão made a sublime no-look pass over to me. "I didn't see Pelé while I was dribbling," he later said, "but I knew where he would be because every time I go to my left he covers the center. I wasn't wrong." I got the ball right in front of the English goal. Instead of shooting, though, I sent a gentle pass wide to my right, evading the two defenders who were closing in on me. Jairzinho, wide-open with only the goalie to beat, took one step and slammed the ball toward the net.

Not even Banks could catch that one. The Mexican crowd went absolutely crazy. Brazil 1, England 0.

That would be the final score—a hard-fought, true team victory. Zagallo, decades later, would still call it "the best match I've ever watched."

Afterward, the Mexicans came to our team hotel to celebrate the victory with us. People were everywhere, hundreds of them—laughing, clapping us on the back, drinking beer and tequila in the hallways and in our rooms. Even the security guard I'd been assigned couldn't keep an eye on everything—at one point, someone sneaked into my room and took all fourteen of my shirts as souvenirs. I didn't really mind, but I was left without anything to wear for the next game! The team even considered asking Bobby Moore, the English player I'd given my shirt to at the end of the game, to give it back. Ultimately, a special airlift from Mexico City solved the problem—and we went back to celebrating.

Like I said—during that era, you just had to embrace the chaos.

16

Our next two games were both very challenging. We worked hard to beat Romania 3–2 in our final game of the group stage, and then we had to face a very spirited team from Peru in the quarter-finals. That game had special meaning for me—the coach for Peru was Didi, my good friend, the "Ethiopian Prince," the elder statesman who had led Brazil to victory in Sweden in 1958. Befitting his own legacy as a player, Didi trained the Peruvian team to play well beyond its natural ability, with a relentless focus on offense. The game we played was free and open, full of attacks and counterattacks—aesthetically speaking, one of the favorite matches I ever played. Brazil won, 4–2.

After vanquishing Peru, all of us gathered in the locker room to listen to the radio. A tightly fought game was taking place in Mexico City to determine who would be facing us in the semifinals. Despite our euphoria at having just won, you could have heard a pin drop in that room. Nobody said a word—in fact, nobody even showered or changed. We were too glued to the action.

Regular time ended with the score tied at zero, so the game went to extra time. Finally, as the overtime drew to a close, one of the teams managed a single goal to win it.

We all looked at one another.

We smiled.

None of us could believe it.

We would be playing Uruguay.

17

A great many things have happened in my life that I don't quite understand. You could call them coincidences, but I don't think that does them justice. No, I believe that, during some moments in our lives, God had his plan. Brazil playing Uruguay in a semifinal, twenty years after the heartbreak at Maracanã, for the first time in a World Cup final since that fateful day in Rio—I don't know how else this can be explained. Now, I don't believe that God necessarily cared about who played who in soccer; I suspect he had more pressing affairs to deal with. But He does send each of us on a journey, so we can grow as individuals and greater appreciate His love. And it seemed only fitting that the young boy who bawled his eyes out that day in Baurú, and promised his dad he'd seek revenge, would now have the opportunity to play Uruguay on soccer's grandest stage. Only God could explain why this happened. One day, I hope to ask Him for a detailed explanation!

Each of us on the team had a very personal connection to that game. Virtually all of us had listened to the action on the radio as kids, and grieved with our families afterward. Zagallo, of course, had even been on the field. Even the younger players—some of whom were barely toddlers on that infamous day—understood the importance of it. And the Brazilian media . . . well, they weren't about to let us forget what this game meant either. Newspapers back home carried the story of a nine-year-old Pelé over and over, turning up the excitement even more.

"Even if we lose the World Cup, we have to beat Uruguay!" I remember one of my teammates saying. "They've been stuck in our throats for twenty years!" another said.

I wish I could say that we all kept our cool. I wish I could say that we ignored the hype, and took the field against Uruguay with the same utter control that characterized our other games in 1970. But that would be a lie. The truth is, we were a total mess. The pressure was unbelievable. And when we took the field, it briefly looked like history might repeat itself in the most horrible way possible.

We came out stumbling, turning the ball over and making errant passes. The Uruguayans had assumed an ultradefensive posture, with ten players back on defense and only one attacker out front. Nevertheless, twenty minutes into the game, Uruguay managed to start the scoring, and took a 1–0 lead. The nervous tittering around radios and TVs back in Brazil started once again—would history repeat itself?

Once again, though, we relied on the strength of one another. The minutes passed, and we calmly passed the ball back and forth. Our composure returned. Some passing space began to open up. We started leaning forward, rather than back on our heels. And just before halftime, Clodoaldo took a great pass from Tostão and tied the game.

After halftime, we came out and were fully ourselves—the group that would go down in soccer history as "The Beautiful Team." We executed our passes, took audacious shots, and anticipated moves way before they happened. In one move that many people remember, I received a fine pass from Tostão and, while streaking down the field, faked out the goalkeeper with a "dummy" move. I had an open, if very difficult, shot on goal. Unfortunately, it went just wide left. It's funny actually—the goals I *didn't* score in 1970 might be more famous than the ones I did! But my teammates picked me up, and put on quite a show. The final score was 3–1.

As we walked off the field together, I felt like a nine-year-old boy again. I had this huge smile, and so did everybody else on the Brazilian team. We all felt as if an injustice from our youths had been put right, twenty years after crying ourselves to sleep as mere boys. It was a tremendous sense of accomplishment, in ways that almost didn't seem rational—like we had vanquished a dragon that had haunted us forever. To make the circle complete, and celebrate in earnest, we'd just need to win one more game.

18

By the final game, we had all been through so much together that it felt like nothing could stop us: not even the feared *azurri* of Italy.

The Italians had a soccer tradition just as rich as ours. Both countries had won two World Cups apiece. In other ways, the Italians were our polar opposite: They played an unapologetically defense-oriented brand of soccer, and had conceded only four goals in the entire World Cup to that point—a span of five games. Some observers found this brand of soccer a bit tough to watch: One English writer called the Italians "forces of darkness" against our "light." But I appreciated their team's toughness, their technical skill and their fans' passion for the game. It was going to be a dream final.

The matchup meant something for history as well. It had been decided years before that, if a country ever won three World Cup titles, they would be able to keep the Jules Rimet trophy permanently. This was an honor, and kind of a neat story as well. Because Italy won the 1938 World Cup, Italy had the trophy in its possession when World War II broke out. The Italian vice president of FIFA, Dr. Ottorino Barassi, hid the trophy in a shoe box under his bed to keep it from falling into the wrong hands. Then, in 1966, the trophy was stolen from a display case in England. A nationwide hunt ended only a week later when a dog named Pickles sniffed under some bushes in London, and found the trophy wrapped in newspapers. As you might imagine, given all the drama over the years, it really meant something that either Brazil or Italy was going to be able to take this storied trophy home and retire it for good.

The day of the match, a driving rainstorm hit Mexico City, stopping only just before the game started. Some people said this might lead to a sloppier, and thus more defense-friendly game, favoring Italy. But luckily the rain did nothing to negate our (by now) not-so-secret weapon: the Mexican crowd. The vast majority of the 107,000 screaming fans at the Azteca Stadium showed up to cheer for us once again, driven not only by their Latin American pride but by a fair dose of resentment: The Italians had eliminated Mexico from the Cup, 4–1.

Once the game got under way, all those external things just disappeared. Our focus was on the field, and one another. Once again, to our utter delight, we played as if perfectly synchronized. After a brilliant move created by Tostão and Rivelino, I jumped—"like a salmon," one newspaper wrote—to reach a high pass by the far post. I was closely guarded by an Italian defender, but all those silly, repetitive drills of Dondinho's paid off in a World Cup game one final time. I hung in the air and nodded my head at just the right moment, putting the ball just past the outstretched hands of the Italian goalie Enrico Albertosi to open the scoring.

Brazil 1, Italy 0.

Italy quickly tied the game, making it 1–1 at halftime. When we went into the locker room, though, we were all business. Nobody really said much—there was no rousing speech. We just trusted in one another, and knew things would break our way if we kept working hard and playing as a team.

Indeed, the second half of the 1970 final was one of the most majestic things I've ever been a part of. All these years later, it makes my skin tingle to think about what happened: the fusion of athletic ability, good coaching and teamwork. For the first twenty minutes of the half, we were pounding, advancing, but couldn't quite break through. Then, finally, a perfect team play: Gérson rolled a pass to Everaldo, who passed to Jairzinho—our feared goal-scoring savant. The Italians converged frantically upon Jairzinho, but he unselfishly found Gérson, who had broken hard toward the goal. Gérson unleashed an unstoppable rocket into the net.

Brazil 2, Italy 1.

Just five minutes later, in the seventy-first minute, Gérson got the action started once again by penetrating the Italian defense. He saw me near the front of the goal and lifted a long, high pass over to me. I leapt into the air like I had in the first half, which scared the Italian goalkeeper. But instead of heading the ball in, I knocked it over to Jairzinho on the other side of the goal. He put the ball in easily—making him the first player ever to score a goal in every game of a World Cup, a record that still stands.

Brazil 3, Italy 1.

Finally, in the eighty-sixth minute, one of the favorite moments of my career. I ended up with the ball in front of the goal once again. Maybe I could have scored on my own, but instead, out of the corner of my eye, I saw Carlos Alberto coming up on my right. Carlos Alberto was my teammate and good friend at Santos, and primarily a defender. He didn't have many chances to score under most circumstances—especially not in a World Cup! But in this case, on this blessed day, Carlos Alberto had an open path to the net. So I flicked a pass over to him, which he duly converted for the final score.

Brazil 4, Italy 1.

For me personally, those goals in the second half made me feel like a cycle had closed. In my first World Cup, in 1958, I was the guy racing ahead toward the net. Now I was in the role Didi had once played—setting up plays for my teammates. I felt enormous pride; this was the player I had always wanted to become.

When the final whistle blew, the crowd stormed the field. They lifted me, Gérson, Jairzinho and Carlos Alberto up on their shoulders and did a lap around the Azteca Stadium. Somehow, a Mexican sombrero found its way onto my head—I kept it, and still have that prized souvenir sitting in my house in Brazil. As far as other clothing goes, my shirt disappeared in the bedlam, but that was about it—and I guess that made me lucky. It was Tostão's turn to end up nearly naked—the crowd stripped him of his jersey, shorts, shoes and even his socks! We all laughed and laughed. Thirty minutes passed before the crowd started to settle down, and we slowly retreated to the locker room.

Nearly everyone agreed: The game was a masterpiece. The Italian coach said afterward: "The Brazilians played as if they had wings." Tarcisio Burgnich, the defender who was charged with shadowing me, said many years later: "I told myself before the game, 'He's made of skin and bones just like everyone else.' But I was wrong." Britain's *Sunday Times*, the same newspaper that described me as a "sad millionaire" after the 1966 Cup, led its next edition with the headline: How do you spell Pelé? G-O-D.

All the vindication felt very sweet. But my favorite moment came in the locker room right after the game. I was sitting there, drinking some water with my teammates, when I felt a mild little tap on my shoulder. I thought it was just another journalist at first, and I didn't look back.

But then Brito said: "Hey, it's Zagallo, man."

I turned around and stood up. There was our coach, standing there, crying tears of joy. For me, he was the one constant—the man who had been there with me for all three of Brazil's championships, first as a teammate and then as my coach. We gave each other a big, long embrace, clapping each other on the back.

"We had to be together to become champions three times," I said, sobbing. "It could only have happened with you. Thank you."

19

That really was the end for me on the national team. After playing a couple more "friendly" games as a farewell in 1971, I stepped away for good.

Once again, politics was a factor in my decision. After we won the 1970 Cup, the military government relentlessly used our victory as a propaganda tool to disguise Brazil's true problems. Meanwhile, the stories we heard about torture and kidnappings multiplied. While I cannot claim that politics was the only reason I retired from the Brazilian team, it certainly was a major element. I couldn't stand the fact that our success was being used to cover up atrocities.

Looking back, I regret that I didn't speak up sooner about the abuses that were going on during the 1960s and 1970s. I think that, throughout my life, my desire to focus on soccer sometimes made me conservative—not in the political sense, but in my willingness to accept the status quo. I was always in a rush to get on the field and play, just as I had been as a kid. I sometimes believed that by choosing not to speak up about our problems, I could keep politics out of soccer, and just concentrate on the game itself. That, of course, was a fantasy.

Many years later, in 2011, I ended up on a plane with Dilma Rousseff, the young leftist militant who, as I mentioned earlier, was being tortured by the military in 1970 as we prepared for the World Cup. Now, of course, Dilma was the democratically elected president of Brazil. She had appointed me as an ambassador for the 2014 World Cup in Brazil, and the conversation turned to our country, and the way it used to be.

"Soccer promoted Brazil, but it also hid a lot of things and covered them up," Dilma told me. "We wanted Brazil to be as good in real life as it was on the soccer field. That's what my comrades and I were fighting for.

"We weren't famous like Pelé," she continued. "So we had to get people's attention through other means.

"Now, here I am today as president. And I'm still trying to make Brazil as good as it can be." She leaned back in her chair and smiled. "I mean, can you understand the series of events that put me here?"

I laughed. "That's something we have in common," I said. "I wonder about those things all the time."

USA, 1994

1

I walked out onto the field, dressed in an all-white suit and a rainbow-colored tie, and felt one of the biggest rushes of my entire life.

Some ninety-four thousand fans were screaming and cheering and waving flags, eager for the 1994 World Cup final to begin. The field was crowded with soldiers, cheerleaders, and delegations and giant flags from all twenty-four countries that had participated in the tournament. On one side, the Brazilian team was warming up, getting ready to play for their first world championship since 1970—a twenty-four-year drought, an eternity by our standards. On the other side, the Italians. It was to be a rematch of that storied Mexico City final that I'd played in, yet another battle royale between perhaps the two greatest powers of global soccer.

But my excitement had little to do with the teams. No, the true miracle was where this World Cup final was taking place: the Rose Bowl, in southern California.

"Ladies and gentlemen," the announcer said, "it is our pleasure to introduce a three-time World Cup winner, who has meant more to the game than any other player. He will be joined today by the world's most popular performer. Here's Whitney Houston, and the great Peléeeeee!"

I joined hands with Whitney, and we ran out onto the field, laughing and smiling at each other. Once we reached the halfway point, she handed me a soccer ball she was carrying in her arms. I punted it as hard as I could into the stands. The crowd went crazy.

As Whitney took the stage to sing, I stood there, euphoric, still not quite able to believe what I was seeing. Here was the world's greatest sport, staging its biggest show in the world's richest country. Just twenty years earlier, nobody would have thought it was possible. Soccer becoming popular in the United States? You would have been more likely to believe that Martians had taken over the earth.

How did this all come to pass? Well, through the hard work of a lot of people. Among them: Mick Jagger, Henry Kissinger, Rod Stewart, a couple of brothers from Armenia, and an American entertainment mogul named Steve Ross, who had a unique, single-minded, borderline crazy vision.

And me, of course.

Yup, it's a pretty wild story!

2

By early 1971, with the chants from the Mexican fans still ringing in my ears, I was ready to start walking away from soccer—this time, for good. I was only thirty-one, but Dondinho and Professor Mazzei had long warned me about the dangers of playing too long. They said it could take a toll on my body, cost me precious time with my family, and distract me from the opportunities that would take up most of my adult years. In other words, it was time to get on with the rest of my life.

In truth, my body felt fine. But, after nearly fifteen years of professional soccer, I was mentally tired—especially because of all the travel. Our son Edinho had been born just six weeks after the 1970 World Cup concluded, and I began to feel an even stronger pull toward home. I knew exactly what it was like to be a young boy in Brazil—I worried that if I wasn't around often enough, he'd lose his way. Meanwhile, Rose was feeling alone and also pent up due to the demands of sports and fame—around that time, she told an interviewer that being in Santos while I was on the road was "like living in a cage."

Thus began the long—and I mean *loooooooong*—good-bye. I said farewell first to the Brazilian national team, as I had planned. The team wanted to hold a few ceremonial matches for me first in both Rio and São Paulo. I agreed, although I had some reservations about drawing things out. With rare exceptions, I hardly ever became nervous before normal competitive games, even World Cup finals. I was so calm, in fact, that I'd often try to take advantage of other players' nerves to try some kind of trick—like the shot from midfield against Czechoslovakia in 1970. But for farewell or homage matches, I was always a bundle of nerves. I can't really explain why. Maybe it was because all the attention in those farewell games was focused solely on me, and the games themselves weren't competitive enough to fully focus my mind on the soccer. Whatever the reason, I felt like a kid waiting for Santa Claus on Christmas Eve. Even stranger: While my memory is generally quite good, I was so uptight during those games that I never remembered a single thing afterward.

In any case, newspaper clippings from the time do, in fact, confirm that the games did happen—including the final "farewell," against Yugoslavia, before one hundred eighty thousand screaming fans at (where else?) the Maracanã in Rio. The game was broadcast all over the world—papers reported that bullfights were even canceled in Seville, Spain, so that people could watch on TV. Inside the stadium, people lit firecrackers and waved white handkerchiefs. When the game ended, I removed my Brazil number ten shirt for the last time and did a lap around the stadium, trailed by a group of junior players who we thought represented the promising next generation for Brazil. The crowd shouted *"Fica! Fica!"* Stay, stay!

Their chant was flattering, and a sign of things to come. Because I'd "retired" and changed my mind once already, in 1966, everybody was certain that I would be a big flake once again. I guess I had only myself to blame! In fact, there would be all kinds of efforts to sway me in time to play in the 1974 World Cup, which was to be held in West Germany. Fans asked me about it everywhere I went. For years, I couldn't do a media interview or go out in public without the question coming up. One lawyer even submitted an affidavit to a Brazilian federal court, saying that because I was "under the jurisdiction" of the

National Sports Confederation, I could be legally *forced* to play for Brazil! That one didn't hold up in court, thankfully. The new Brazilian head of FIFA, João Havelange, kept after me until just a few months before the 1974 Cup, when he sent me a letter, which he made public, urging me to "revise" my decision in time for the tournament.

"I am hoping," Havelange wrote, "for the word of encouragement which will make hope spring like flourishing greenery across the verdant fields made fertile by the fervor that the Brazilian people have devoted to the sport in which you have become an idol."

Wow! That was a hard one to say no to. Zagallo, my friend and coach from 1970, also asked me to reconsider, saying I was just the missing piece Brazil needed in the attack. Turning up the pressure even more, the new head of the military government, President Ernesto Geisel, declared publicly that he wanted me back on the national team. When I still wouldn't budge, President Geisel's own daughter paid me a visit in Santos. "It would mean a lot for Brazil, and my father, if you played in 1974," she said. "It would be good for the country."

I was really very flattered by such requests, but my answer remained firm: No, thank you. I had my reasons for retiring—both personal and political ones, as I've said. I had the great fortune of playing in four World Cups, and the last one was the best. All told, I had scored seventy-seven goals for the Brazilian team throughout my career, a national record that still stands. I really was finished. It was a true honor to represent Brazil, and I would continue to do so with great pride for the rest of my life. But not as a player for the national team.

Once I departed the national team, I still had two years left on my contract with Santos. The team's glory days of the 1960s had passed—many of my old friends, such as Pepe and Gylmar Santos, had retired. We seemed to have a different coach each day. The club even made the terrible mistake of firing my closest friend and adviser, Professor Mazzei. One newspaper described us in 1972 as a "once-great team that used to play attractive soccer." That was a bit harsh, perhaps, but the author had a point. In 1973, we even lost to a third-division English club, Plymouth Argyle, by a 3–2 score. Meanwhile, Santos seemed determined to squeeze out every last dime it could before I left. In the eighteen months prior to my departure, we toured South America, the Caribbean, North America, Europe, Asia and Australia. I think Timbuktu may have been the only place we didn't play. Never in my life had I traveled so much—it was exactly the opposite of what I hoped for following Edinho's birth. I'd played more than a thousand games for Santos by that point, and the constant travel only confirmed my resolve—it was time to go.

Nevertheless, the good-bye tour for Santos was just as emotional as the one for the national team, if not more so. For me, one of the most touching moments was my last game against Corinthians. I had always seemed to find an extra gear when playing the "Timão," the "big team," as it's called, and I scored forty-nine goals in forty-nine games against them during my career—a pretty high ratio. Usually, when we played them, I was one hundred percent focused on scoring goals and celebrating another win. But that day, when I arrived at the stadium in São Paulo for my finale against them, I was overwhelmed to see Corinthians fans waving banners with my name and cheering me, as if I were one of them. The club even set a new record for ticket sales at that game. It reminded me of how, while our biggest opponents loved their teams, they *loved* the game of soccer above all. That love was something that united fans and players, no matter what team or country they played for.

The final game for Santos was against a team from São Paulo state called Ponte Preta. I was actually hurting quite a lot—stress probably played a role, to be honest—and I did all kinds of rehab to be ready to take the field one last time. I could barely walk. Once the game began, though, I felt better. I didn't know exactly how I would say farewell to the crowd until about twenty minutes into the game, when I was standing in midfield, and one of my Santos teammates lofted a pass over to me.

Rather than chest the ball down to the ground, as I would have normally done, I caught the ball with my hands—the ultimate no-no in soccer. The crowd gasped. The other players stared at me, dumbfounded.

That was my way of saying—That's it, folks. It's over.

I jogged over to the center of the field, the ball still in my hands, tears rolling down my face. Then I knelt down and spread out my arms, like a big hug. I wanted to thank all the people there, all the supporters, all Brazilians and, of course, God. I was a few weeks shy of my thirty-fourth birthday—and convinced that I would never play professional soccer again.

As the *New York Times* wrote the next day: "Pelé, the magic Brazilian forward generally considered to be the world's best soccer player, has begun the slow change that will make him Edson Arantes do Nascimento, the rich young Brazilian businessman, pleasant hunting and fishing companion, and devoted husband and father of two children."

Well . . . that was the idea.

3

For the first few weeks after I retired from Santos, people talked about me as if I had died. Friends, former teammates, journalists and others came over to our house in Santos and said not to worry, they'd still come and see me every now and then. Everybody asked me if I was OK. Of course I was OK, I told them! But people kept asking the question so often that I started to wonder: Was I really OK?

Rose and I, eager to start leading a "normal" life, tried going to restaurants in and around Santos. This was pretty audacious—with rare exceptions, we hadn't done this for a decade, for fear of getting mobbed by well-wishers. Even in retirement, going out on the town took some persistence. The first time we went someplace new, we would in fact be swarmed with people. They came over to our table and wanted to chat about my three goals against France in 1958, about Garrincha, about whether my right foot or left foot was stronger . . . and so on. I was perfectly happy to sit there and relive these moments with them all night. But it wasn't why we went out, and Rose would understandably get a bit cross. Still, we kept at it, and if we went to a restaurant a second time, people would usually just limit themselves to asking for autographs. And the third time, maybe they'd just wave from a distance.

I tried to split my time between my family and attending to my businesses. One afternoon, my business partner Edvar came to pick me up for a trip to São Paulo. As I was leaving the house, my daughter, Kely Cristina, ran up to me and said: "So, Dad, you're going out *again*?"

I stood there, silent, not quite knowing how to respond.

Edvar finally spoke up. "Well, yes, that's true. But you know, Kely, since he's stopped playing, he's going to have a lot more time to spend with you."

Kely put her hands on her hips. "Um, I'll just wait and see about that!"

She was only seven. But she knew her dad. Maybe even better than I did.

4

made every effort to line up a good post-soccer life. That included doing something that would have absolutely horrified the nine-year-old Edson: going back to school. Ever since my childhood, my family, friends and mentors had been talking to me about my lack of a formal education. They all agreed it would come back to haunt me one day—regardless of whether I was the world's most famous athlete or not. Waldemar de Brito, my youth coach from Baurú, was especially adamant. "Dico," he'd say, "you were born to play soccer, there's no doubt. But your career is going to end when you're at the very best moment of your life. And then you'll need school!"

I was also aware of the fact that kids all over the world looked up to me. I embraced the responsibility that came with being a role model. What kind of message did it send, then, that Pelé had never finished high school? Everyone knew this about me, everywhere around the world, and I felt embarrassed, like I had let everyone down. Around that time, a magazine in Switzerland generated some buzz when it published a caricature of me on the cover, and the caption: "We parents must soon ask ourselves whether there is any sense in letting our sons study."

As I neared age thirty, and I started thinking more about what my life would look like after soccer, I realized that time was running out for me to address this problem. It felt like something basic in my life was missing. In my travels over the years, I had met all kinds of inspiring people: popes and professors, politicians and doctors. I tried so hard to keep up with them, but sometimes it was difficult to know what they were saying. I didn't think I was lacking in intelligence or good instincts; but I did lack a formal education, and I knew that would only damage me more as time went by. So, I decided that I would get a physical education degree from a university in Santos. This wouldn't be *that* big of a stretch—after all, it was the same field I'd been working in for the last fifteen years! But of course getting a university degree meant that I'd first have to learn all the things I missed in high school.

So, while still playing for Santos, I spent my off days, and a lot of nights after games, studying as hard as I could. This was a massive challenge—to be honest, when I first started playing soccer in the 1950s, I barely knew how to sign my name for autographs. But Professor Mazzei was constantly looking over my shoulder, helping me with the lessons and encouraging me, like he always did.

I overcame my nerves and passed the exam, and got my high school diploma. I was very proud, but there was no real time to celebrate—I spent another whole year preparing for the entrance exam for college, which included Brazilian history, math and a physical endurance test. Now, you would think the final subject would have been the easiest for me, but when the time came, I almost failed! Why? Well, the test included a twenty-five-yard swimming exercise. I'd spent all that time fishing in the Baurú River as a child, but had never actually learned to swim in it. I nearly drowned that day!

After three years of hard work, I got my degree. In the end, I was so glad I did it. Not so much for the kids, for the fans, or for my mentors. I did it for me. It made me a better man.

5

Man, if only I'd mastered math a few years earlier.

Shortly after my final game with Santos, we brought in some auditors to have a complete look at my portfolio. I had tried to be prudent over the years, investing large chunks of the money I made from playing soccer and endorsements, instead of blowing the cash on a lot of cars and houses. I had never forgotten that an athlete's career could end at any time, and I didn't want to have to worry about my finances once I retired. I had accumulated local businesses and properties, and had greatly diversified my investments, just as people insisted I should. Now that my playing career was finally over, I would finally have the time to dedicate myself fully to my businesses. So why not get a full panorama of what I owned, and what it was all worth?

I can still remember the sweat on the accountant's brow when he walked into my office. He looked like he was about to pass out. I immediately sensed something was wrong, and I tried to lighten the mood with good cheer.

"So," I said, smiling, "how many millions have we got?"

The accountant turned even paler! I should have called him a doctor right then and there.

"It's complicated," he said.

Actually, it wasn't very complicated at all. I wasn't worth millions. I *owed* millions. While I had accumulated a wide range of assets, I hadn't paid much attention to what they were—I allowed other people to do that for me. There was one company that completely canceled out all the good things we had done. It was called Fiolax, a parts manufacturer. Unwisely, I had signed a note guaranteeing a bank loan for the company as well as its liabilities, even though I wasn't a majority shareholder. When the company couldn't pay the loan, the bank came after me. There was also a fine because the company had violated some import regulations. All told, the company owed several million dollars, and I was the one stuck with the bill.

You might ask: Edson, how could you have been so stupid? Well, the better question would be: How could you have been so stupid *twice*? I'm sad to say it wasn't even the first time this had happened to me. About a decade earlier, in the mid-1960s, I had also suddenly discovered I was deep in debt. On that occasion, I had signed over my power of attorney to a man I thought was my friend, and who had vowed to take care of my business affairs for me. One day, a few months before my wedding to Rose, he came to me and asked for money—which I thought was a little weird, since I had already given him plenty. That led to a series of questions and investigations, which ended in the discovery that I was penniless.

The two episodes had a lot in common. In both cases, I had trusted people who I believed were my friends, but mainly wanted money and recognition for themselves. In both cases, my desire to focus on soccer—and soccer alone—led me to be careless and stupid with my money. In both cases, some people urged me to just declare bankruptcy and walk away from the bad loans. And in both cases, I decided that it was important to honor my debts in full. I did this partly because I wanted to set a good example, and partly because it was all so very embarrassing. No one would believe that Pelé, of all the people in the world, was really broke—they would assume I was perpetrating some dishonest scam.

Nowadays, the story of professional athletes who squander their fortune seems as old as the Bible itself. Back then, though, it was pretty much unthinkable. If I was one of the first global sports superstars to make millions from endorsements, I was also one of the first to lose everything he had. There was no instruction manual or guidebook on how to deal with this, no wise elders whom I could turn to for support. No one was sympathetic—in fact, some people seemed to take a strange pleasure in the misfortune that had befallen me, an emotion that I have personally never understood. My situation was unique, and I would have to deal it with myself.

The first time it happened, I went to the board of Santos Football Club and asked them for money to pay off my short-term debts. They agreed, as long as I agreed to sign a new contract that was favorable to the club. I had no choice but to accept. Over the course of several years, I was able to pay off the money I owed. With the help of several endorsement deals, I started building up my equity again, step by step. Until, of course, the walls crashed down around me a second time.

So—how could I earn the money back now? Well, clearly, I wasn't great at business. That much was clear! Thankfully, though, there was something left in this world I was still pretty good at.

6

The first time I heard of the New York Cosmos was at a post-championship party in 1970 in Mexico City, when I met two brothers from Armenia. The Erteguns told me a little bit about their desire to start a soccer team in New York City. "We're in the world's greatest city, and we're going to create the world's best soccer team," one of them said. It was an interesting concept, but I must admit that I promptly forgot about the whole thing. It seemed like one of those crazy ideas you hear at a party, when everyone has had just a little too much to drink.

The Cosmos weren't officially created until the following year, 1971—and for a while, the club seemed destined to fail. The team played in the North American Soccer League, which was the second attempt to organize professional soccer in the United States. The Cosmos had a staff of just five people, and a top wage for players of seventy-five dollars per game. On a very good day, they were drawing five thousand people to their games, which were played on a ragged soccer field on Randalls Island, a tiny sliver of land between Manhattan and Queens in New York City. The players had day jobs in construction, restaurants or as taxi drivers. Really, it was a semiprofessional league, one that was living on a hand-to-mouth basis, its future totally uncertain.

Soccer in the United States had always been a tough sell. Americans seemed to think soccer was "foreign" or "elitist." I never understood this stigma, which didn't seem to exist anywhere else in the world. As I've said, soccer is the most egalitarian of games, one that anybody can start playing right away. Regardless of how much money you have, how big you are, how fast you can run, or how many friends you can find, you can always be playing soccer in just two seconds. In contrast, some of the most popular American sports—football, baseball and golf, to name a few—require lots of expensive equipment, and often a specially designed playing field. And *soccer* was supposedly elitist?

Looking back, I think the biggest problem for American soccer was a more sensible one: The quality wasn't very good. Americans always want the best, and they usually got it when they watched baseball, basketball, boxing, ice hockey or football. They could turn on their TV or go to a stadium and see Joe Namath, Hank Aaron, Muhammad Ali or Kareem Abdul-Jabbar. But when they went to a professional soccer game, they usually got some Italian, Colombian or Polish guy whom they'd never heard of before, and who wasn't even in the world's top echelon of players. Watching a mediocre product wasn't much fun. Of course, there was a chicken-and-the-egg element to this: Few Americans liked soccer, so few Americans played it all that well, so few Americans liked it, and so on.

The problems faced by the professional soccer leagues reflected this vicious cycle. Bill MacPhail, the head of CBS Sports during that era, reflected on why the first professional soccer league failed, even with the money that came from its television broadcast deal: "The stadiums were empty, which made it tough for us to generate much excitement," MacPhail said. "The players had foreign names, their faces were unfamiliar, their backgrounds undistinguished." Because the action was so uninspiring, some fans couldn't be bothered to learn the finer points of what makes soccer worthwhile, just as someone exposed only to garage bands wouldn't appreciate Bach or Beethoven. As the U.S. magazine

Sports Illustrated wrote in 1972: "A typical American crowd might ignore a skillful pass or dribble, then cheer a 30- or 40-yard kick that misses the goal, just as a European might cheer a long foul in baseball."

Still, there was promise. You had to search for it, sure, but it was there. For one thing, the history of U.S. soccer was not quite as barren as most people thought. During the 1950 World Cup, Uruguay beating Brazil at the Maracanã wasn't even the biggest upset of the tournament. The United States shocked England, the birthplace of modern soccer, by a score of 1–0 before a crowd of some ten thousand people in Belo Horizonte, Brazil. The winning goal was scored by Joe Gaetjens, a Haitian-born man who was working in the United States at the time, and was allowed to play for the national team because he had expressed his intent to become a U.S. citizen. (He never actually did.) The result was such a shock that, when *The New York Times* received a wire-service account of the final score, they didn't immediately publish it, thinking it was a hoax. Writing about the game fifty years later, the *Times* said it remained "one of the sport's greatest upsets."

Four decades would pass until the Americans again attained similar success at the World Cup. But, in the meantime, other interesting things were also happening. At the college level, the game was gaining some converts. Thanks in part to the social changes happening in the United States in the 1960s and 1970s, girls and women were beginning to embrace soccer, to a much greater extent than in Europe or South America. Also important, there was a group of very powerful people in business and media who were starting to take a keen interest in soccer as well.

One of them was Steve Ross. Steve was the chairman of Warner Communications, and a man who spent his entire life taking big risks and innovating. His empire included Atlantic Records, with artists such as Led Zeppelin and Crosby, Stills and Nash; Hollywood studios with talent such as Steven Spielberg and Robert Redford; and even a company, Atari, that made these new things called "video games." Ross first took an interest in soccer through the Ertegun brothers, who ran Atlantic. Before long, Steve became obsessed with the idea of making soccer popular in the United States.

Why? Of all the "toys" that Steve had at his disposal, with all the access to celebrities and music and the arts, why would soccer, of all things, become the object of his affection? Years later, Steve explained it to me. He said he used to have the same prejudices against the game as most Americans: It was too slow, too "foreign," too difficult to understand what was really going on. But once he started watching the game, and had some friends explain it to him, he realized how fascinating soccer could be. He believed that it just needed the right conditions to thrive. In other words, he saw soccer like an entrepreneur, which of course was exactly what he was, and an excellent one at that. He spotted an unmet need, an undervalued asset, and made it his personal mission to make it succeed, come hell or high water.

After the Cosmos struggled through its first few seasons, switching stadiums every so often and failing to generate much buzz, Steve purchased the team from its original investors for the grand price of one dollar. And then, for no good reason other than his own passion and drive, Steve decided to throw the entire commercial and marketing weight of Warner Communications behind the team. He would not only make the Cosmos a winner, but bring a "new" spectator sport to the American public.

Steve Ross and his staff believed in soccer. They knew the game itself was a winner. They just believed that, in order to make it popular, they needed to improve the quality of play. To make that happen, they believed they needed a name-brand star. And they had heard of some guy down in Brazil who was apparently pretty good.

7

The idea didn't appeal much to me at first.

Well, let's be honest: It was absurd!

The Cosmos' general manager, a former British sportswriter named Clive Toye, started trying to recruit me as far back as 1971, the year after the World Cup in Mexico. I was still with Santos at the time, and Clive came to the team hotel while we were playing a game in Jamaica. He tracked me down by the pool, where I was sitting in a lounge chair with Professor Mazzei.

"We want you to bring soccer to America," Clive said, practically too nervous to breathe. "We think you're just the man to do it. Money's no object."

Clive outlined some basic terms of the offer. He sat there talking while Professor Mazzei translated. I have to admit, during that first visit, I was only half listening. I wasn't trying to be rude, but you have to understand—I had been receiving offers to play outside Brazil for more than a decade by that point. Many of the best teams of Europe, including AC Milan and Real Madrid, had made fevered overtures over the years. I was flattered, of course, but every time speculation about my departure heated up, the Brazilian press would go absolutely crazy.

This was before the era when the best South American players made a habit of playing in Europe—all eleven of the starters on the 1970 national team played for Brazilian clubs, believe it or not. So many commentators accused me of being an opportunist or even a national traitor, in tune with the "Brazil: Love It or Leave It" philosophy that characterized Brazil during those dictatorship years. The media weren't the only ones who got excited—at one point, the Brazilian government even declared me a "national treasure," which some people said would prevent me from leaving Brazil to play abroad.

The funny thing was, I had never seriously entertained the notion of playing soccer outside Brazil. I had my reasons: In a nutshell, I really loved my mom's *arroz e feijão*, her homemade rice and beans. I guess that's a Brazilian way of saying that I'm very happy and comfortable at home, and I always have been. Without leaving Santos, I could play for what was, for many years, the world's best soccer club. I had my mom and dad in a house just a few blocks away from our apartment. Rose and the kids were very happy in Santos. It was always eighty degrees, and a glorious beach was right there for the taking. Playing for the Brazilian national team, and for Santos on our frequent trips abroad, gave me plenty of opportunities to measure my abilities against quality opponents in Europe and elsewhere. So, sure, why on earth would I ever leave?

Even if I did get the urge to wander, and play soccer elsewhere, the United States hardly seemed like the first place I'd go. Don't get me wrong—I loved the country itself. I loved the freedom: the freedom to raise your family in peace, the freedom to do business and make money, the freedom to walk around without fearing for your safety. It was a place where you could pursue your own dreams without anybody—the government, the business elite—standing in your way. This may sound very basic to Americans, but for a Brazilian, and for people from many other countries, it was an amazing revelation. I remember visiting Los Angeles with Rose during the late 1960s, and we went down to Hollywood Boulevard. As we walked around, I became intoxicated by how prosperous and peaceful everything seemed. Being able to walk down a street without being overwhelmed by people was a plus, too. I swept Rose into my arms, lifted her high into the air and began shouting: "I'm free! I'm free!"

But American soccer? It seemed like a nut that couldn't be cracked. The Cosmos seemed to have more in common with an amateur team than the high-level competition I was accustomed to in Brazil or in Europe. And despite all of Clive's promises, I was skeptical of the very American-seeming notion that whatever you didn't have, you could buy. How would bringing me to the United States magically create interest in a country that already had four top-rate professional sports leagues? It seemed ridiculous.

I, too, was underestimating the power of soccer.

8

─────────

Clive Toye kept after me for years, obsessively, like some kind of crazy hunter—I was Moby-Dick to his Captain Ahab. He even made the Cosmos' team colors yellow and green, the same colors that the Brazilian national team used, thinking that this might help seduce me. No matter how many times I politely told him no, or how clearly I said I would never ever *ever* leave Brazil, he would always show up again, lurking in a hotel lobby or making his way to the sidelines of my games. Each time, he acted as if the conversation was the first we'd ever had. "We have this great team we're putting together in New York," he'd begin, just as earnestly as the first time we talked. "We think you should come play with us for three years."

I'd smile, and listen, but I also didn't want to give him false hopes. "Thank you, but I'm very happy in Brazil," I'd say. "And in 1974, I will retire from Santos and from soccer."

That's precisely what I did, of course. Even then, Clive kept asking. And I kept turning him down—until I started to think, hmm, maybe playing in New York City wasn't such a crazy idea after all.

I won't try to disguise this: A big reason for my change of heart was the ill-fated visit from the accountant in late 1974. I owed millions, I was determined to pay the debt, and I knew that playing soccer was by far the best way for me to do so. The sums that Clive was mentioning amounted to the most lucrative sports contract in history, in any sport. But there were other reasons, too, that had absolutely nothing to do with money.

One of Clive's best lines had to do with the unique opportunity of bringing soccer to the United States. "Play for Real Madrid and you might win a championship," he would say. "Play for New York, and you'll win a country." This overture resonated with me a lot, actually—the Cosmos were offering an opportunity to not just play soccer, but to change its whole culture in one of the world's greatest and most important countries.

This was important, and not just for the United States, I believed. Finally getting Americans on board with soccer would have a positive effect everywhere. After all, the U.S. was home not only to millions of wealthy fans, but also to Hollywood and most of the world's biggest companies. Through my sponsorships with Pepsi and other companies, I had seen firsthand how U.S. corporate money could be used to do good in the world, by funding soccer clinics and building facilities in poor neighborhoods, for example. During those years, I also saw how companies were more and more interested in developing markets and opportunities beyond their home territory. It was clear that this was a tremendous force. If we could get the American people interested in soccer, then American companies would follow. That, in turn, would be good for soccer players in Brazil as well as countless other countries. This was all a huge challenge, but I knew that if I succeeded, it would be something I could be proud of forever.

The possibility of living in the United States also appealed greatly to my newest passion: education. Our kids were still young enough to learn fluent English, which I knew would serve them well for the rest of their lives. Rose said she was excited about the possibility of residing in another country, and exploring a world beyond Santos. I also knew that living in the world's richest country would teach me a few lessons about how business works. Who knew? Maybe I'd finally acquire the ability to earn millions of dollars without promptly losing them.

Another plus: a small degree of anonymity. I had played a few ex-hibition games with Santos in the United States as part of our global tours, and there were quite a lot of people who recognized me there. I'd even been named an honorary citizen of Kansas City after Santos played there in the early seventies! But it wasn't like elsewhere in the world, where seemingly *everyone* knew exactly who I was, usually from a hundred yards away. In America, even some "soccer people" often mispronounced my name, calling me "Peel." I wouldn't have wanted to go somewhere where I was completely unknown—that would have de-feated the purpose—but the United States seemed to offer a happy medium between anonymity and the usual crush of fans. After all, the United States already had so many famous people in movies and sports. And if the idea of moving to New York City to get some peace and quiet sounds odd . . . well, anybody who followed my life for the previous twenty years would have understood.

Finally, sometimes the little experiences that happen to us in life, and the people we come across, can have a huge effect on our decisions. One morning in Brussels, Belgium, Clive showed up—lurking, smiling, in a good mood, as always—at my hotel. I had retired from Santos by this time, and had played the night before in a charity game for the retiring Belgian captain, the great Paul Van Himst. Clive invited him-self into my room, and kept having to start his pitch over as a proces-sion of international soccer superstars—guys like Rivelino of Brazil and Eusebio of Portugal—barged in to hug me good-bye.

"Come on, Pelé, just three years," Clive was pleading.

By that point, I had *some* interest in what this man was saying. But I remember that particular day I was in a hurry to leave Belgium and get back to my family in Brazil. Such a hurry, in fact, that as I leaned down to pick up my suitcase, I tore a giant hole in the seat of my pants!

I called downstairs to the lobby and asked if they had anybody who could quickly sew the hole closed. They sent up a maid, who collected the pants and disappeared. Clive was still making his case when, a few minutes later, there was a knock on the door.

It was the maid again. She held the pants in one hand, and a cam-era in the other. Tears were streaming down her cheeks.

She stepped into the room, shaking, and handed the camera to Clive. "Please, sir," she whispered hoarsely, "would you take a picture of me with Pelé?"

The maid—whose name, I'm ashamed to say, I don't recall—told me that her husband had bought a ticket to the previous night's game. He had been hoping to see me play for the first time. Two weeks before the game, sadly, he died of a heart attack. So her son used the ticket, and went to the game instead. The maid wanted a photo of me so she could give it to her son as a kind of memorial.

Halfway through her story, I was already crying. By the time she finished, I was shuddering with sobs. The story was tragic, and I felt profound sympathy for this woman and her son. Also, her story reminded me of the profound connections I'd forged with so many people over the years as a soccer player. I had been retired for a few months by this point, but that old feeling washed over me: warm, sentimental, alive. It reminded me of my true place in this world. And I realized that, for all my misgivings over the years about fame, I desperately missed the most basic and rewarding part of being an athlete—the bond with my fans. It wasn't too late to try to recapture it.

After the maid finished telling the story, and Clive took several pictures of her and me together, I kissed her good-bye and she left the room. Then I turned to Clive.

"OK," I said. "I'll play for the Cosmos."

Clive's eyes lit up like a child on Christmas morning. "Really?"

I nodded, smiling.

He started running around the room—frantic, in jerks and stops, totally unsure how to react. It was as if he'd never considered the possibility I might say yes! What to do now? I really liked Clive by this point, so I told him to just relax and do what he needed to do.

Finally, he had me sign a little piece of hotel stationery, expressing my intent to play for the team. It wasn't quite that simple, of course— we'd need to negotiate a real contract, with agents and intermediaries and all those things. But the signed sheet of paper was a start. Many years later, Clive still had it hanging in a frame in his office—G.B. Motor Inn, Brussels, the letterhead read.

Imagine: Me, a poor kid from Brazil, talked out of retirement by a British man working for an American soccer club—with a Belgian woman delivering the coup de grâce! This was no longer the world as I had first seen it, as a starry-eyed teenager in Sweden in 1958. All of a sudden, everything seemed to be more connected—money and people were flowing around the globe in search of one another. Today, they call this "globalization," and although we didn't have a snappy name for it in the mid-1970s, it was changing the way people made decisions and interacted with one another. Basically, it meant that if Steve Ross and Warner Communications wanted to do whatever it took to get a famous Brazilian soccer player to play for their little team in New York, nothing was going to get in their way.

In retrospect, I didn't stand a chance!

9

For the press conference to announce my arrival, the Cosmos rented out the 21 Club, a glamorous nightclub frequented by celebrities in Manhattan. Some three hundred members of the media (and more than a few curious spectators) showed up—double the club's capacity, and almost as many people as had attended some of the club's games. I was a little late, unfortunately, and as the crowd grew tense, a fistfight broke out among the reporters. A Brazilian cameraman had his glasses broken. The police briefly threatened to call the whole thing off.

Why was it so chaotic? Well, it was New York City in the 1970s! It was a time of soaring crime and blackouts and open-air drug use and gritty streets, back when Times Square was a hotbed of adult cinemas instead of the glowing neon retail theme park of today. It was an era before security became king, before economic growth "cured" many ills, when it seemed like chaos was lurking behind every corner. It was, in other words, a lot like Brazil! I was going to feel right at home.

Despite all the buzz, my transfer almost didn't happen. Getting from the little sheet of paper in the Belgian hotel to the 21 Club was an odyssey that involved numerous late-night negotiations, transcontinental flights and miles of telex tape (a since-forgotten system of rapid communication, technologically somewhere between the telegraph and texting). Delegates from Warner Communications, representing Steve Ross, came to Brazil and at one point we played soccer for a few hours on the beach in Rio as we tried to iron out the details.

Not even that got us a breakthrough. Six months passed with no deal. At one point, it seemed like the negotiations were stuck. We couldn't quite agree on money. Also, the Brazilian military government was making noises about whether it was a good idea for Pelé to play abroad. You have to remember, this was an era when Brazil was still a quite isolated country, paranoid about its security and closed to the world in trade and many other things. "Globalization" was something the government feared, rather than embraced, because they knew that more exposure to the world would make Brazilians demand democracy and other rights. The military, just like all authoritarian regimes, had erected lots of barriers to keep this from happening. So, it seemed entirely possible that the soldiers who ran Brazil might act to stop me from playing in the United States, of all places. Moreover, many of those same soldiers were still angry about my decision not to play for Brazil in 1974, a choice that of course had a political element to it. While it wasn't clear exactly how they'd stop me from leaving if I wanted to play abroad, this being Brazil, there were any number of legal tricks at the government's disposal to keep me at home. I wondered if the whole thing was going to fall apart.

Enter Henry Kissinger. The German-born secretary of state was one of the most powerful Cabinet secretaries in the history of the United States—and a *huge* soccer fan. He had played the game in his youth—as a goalie, of all things—and never lost his passion for the game. In 1973, he used some of his considerable clout to almost single-handedly orchestrate an exhibition game between Santos and the Baltimore Bays, another team in the NASL (and, not coincidentally, one that played close enough to Washington for him to come see the game!). He sought me out in the locker room after that 1973 game, looking like a wide-eyed kid. He told me that only star players would make Americans appreciate the true beauty of soccer. "Pelé, you are the one," he said in his deep, gravelly, heavily accented voice. "We need you to play in the United States more often. People will go crazy. And even if soccer doesn't catch on, at least I'll be able to see you play!"

That same summer, Dr. Kissinger arranged for Rose and me to make a quick visit to the White House, where I met President Nixon. It's funny—I had forgotten about that meeting until recently, when the very last set of the secret tape recordings Nixon made in the Oval Office was released to the public, and I was on them! President Nixon was very polite, and said he thought I was "the greatest in the world." At one point he asked me if I spoke any Spanish.

"No," I said gently. "Only Portuguese."

Nixon looked just a bit embarrassed, so I quickly added:

"It's all the same, though."

By the time Dr. Kissinger heard the Cosmos were negotiating to sign me in early 1975, President Nixon was gone—he had resigned because of Watergate. But Dr. Kissinger had survived, and was just as powerful as ever. He resolved to do whatever was necessary to grease the wheels so I could play in New York. In that spirit, he sent a letter to Brazilian president Ernesto Geisel, stating that if I played in the United States, it would be a massive boost to relations between our two countries. This was during the Cold War—this was Henry Kissinger. Well, you can imagine the effect the letter had. After that, the government grumblings about my impending departure abruptly stopped. We came to an agreement on money—about a million dollars a year for seven years. It was a deal that included all kinds of merchandising and promotion deals as well. One condition was bringing Professor Mazzei, who was hired by the Cosmos to be the assistant coach and fitness adviser. And before I knew it, there I was, standing at a podium at the 21 Club, with the good professor translating for me.

"You can spread the word," I declared. "Soccer has finally arrived in the United States."

It all sounded great, but there was one question nobody knew the answer to: Would anyone actually come and watch us play?

10

'm not even sure I wanted to watch in the beginning!

On the day of my first workout with the Cosmos, there was a driving rainstorm. The chauffeur didn't even know how to get to the workout site—a small gym at Hofstra University, a school on Long Island. So I was nearly an hour late. This sent a horrible message—the last thing I wanted to do was create the impression that I thought I was operating under a different set of rules from my teammates. So I apologized profusely to Coach Bradley. He said it wasn't a problem, and he even generously waived the customary twenty-five dollar fine for players who showed up late.

I gathered the team together and I gave a short speech in my very awful English. I had practiced a bit beforehand with Professor Mazzei, who helped with my pronunciation. I rehearsed a bit that morning in the mirror, too.

"It's an honor to be here," I said. "I've always been a team guy, and I still am. Please don't expect me to win games alone. We must work together."

The guys on the team all nodded. They came up and introduced themselves one by one, smiling and very graciously welcoming me. It was very important for me to learn their names right away. One of my new teammates, Gil Mardarescu, a midfielder from Romania, made the sign of a cross on his chest and said: "I dreamed of one day just shaking your hand. But to play with you, this is a miracle!"

I was flattered, of course. But this was also the kind of starstruck attitude we had to avoid on the field—as I had told the team, our team couldn't be ten guys and Pelé. Soccer doesn't work that way. I became even more worried.

When we all got on the field together for the first time, the result was pretty shaky. I hadn't played competitive soccer in eight months at that point, and I knew I would be rusty. There was also a bit of standing around and gaping while I went through drills and practice kicks. "The Cosmos acted like a sandlot baseball team suddenly playing alongside Babe Ruth," one reporter wrote. I had arrived in the middle of the 1975 season, and the team's record was just three wins, six losses. The players' attitudes were good, but we needed more talent. At that first practice, we were playing an intrasquad game when I received a waist-high pass in front of the goal. I did a bicycle kick, launching the ball past the goalie, Kurt Kuykendall, and into the net.

It was a move I'd performed a thousand times in Brazil, but Kuykendall acted as if he'd just seen a man walk on the moon. "What happened?" he kept asking. "What just happened?" Players on both sides were cheering me, clapping me on the back.

We needed time together. But there wasn't any—it was midseason, after all, and we had a game to play on June 15 against the Dallas Tornadoes. The site would be Downing Stadium, the tattered little venue on Randalls Island where the Cosmos had been playing its home games. The game would be carried live on national television—a first for the Cosmos. Before kickoff, a group of team officials carefully combed over the field, busily working to prepare the facility for its big-time debut. Of course, we had no idea whether anyone would watch on TV or even come to the game itself—the Cosmos' average attendance that year had been just under nine thousand fans a game.

I was delighted when we took the field and saw some twenty-one thousand fans—basically, the little field's capacity. "Pelé! Pelé!" they chanted. At first, it seemed like we might disappoint them—the Tornadoes scored two goals in the first half. Every time I got the ball, three or four defenders came my way. But shortly after halftime, I was able to get a pass to Mordechai Spiegler, our Israeli forward who had played for his national team in the 1970 Cup. He quickly made the score 2–1. Nine minutes later, Spiegler returned the favor, sending a high ball in front of the goal. I jumped up—not quite as high as in my glory days, but enough altitude for that day—and delivered a header into the upper left part of the goal. "Pelé! Pelé!" The chants intensified, and I felt for a moment like I was back at the Vila Belmiro Stadium in Santos.

The final score: 2–2. A tie. Not the kind of result that Americans typically like, but a good start nonetheless.

In fact, we had only one real problem that day. After my postgame shower, I found Raphael de la Sierra, the Cuban-born vice president of the Cosmos. I have to admit, I was in a panic.

"I'm very sorry," I said. "But I think this will be both the first and last game I play for the New York Cosmos. I can't do this."

De la Sierra stared at me with his mouth gaping. "But why?"

I was horrified to discover in the shower that my feet were covered in what looked like green fungus. No matter how much I scrubbed, how much soap I applied, the stuff wouldn't come off. This was my worst fear come true—a facility so decrepit that it would cause me permanent damage to my health. No soccer player can live without his feet.

As I explained myself, de la Sierra's frown disappeared, and soon he was smiling. He patiently waited for me to finish speaking. Then he informed me that, because Downing Stadium had been in such awful condition prior to the game, team officials had spray-painted several huge bald spots of the soccer field with green paint. They did this hoping that the viewers on television wouldn't be able to tell the difference, and would think the Cosmos played its games on a beautiful, lush field.

"That's not fungus, Pelé," he said, quaking with laughter. "That was paint."

11

That first game attracted a television audience of ten million people—easily a record for soccer in the United States, beating any World Cup or club game up until that point. The broadcast itself wasn't a total success—the TV audience missed the first Cosmos goal because of a commercial break, as well as the second one, which I scored, because they were showing an instant replay at the time. Clearly, soccer, with its constant action, contrasting with the long, TV-friendly pauses seen in most "American" sports, was going to pose a learning curve for everyone—even the TV executives!

Nevertheless, the reviews were overwhelmingly positive. "Except for a heavyweight championship fight," one newspaper wrote, "no sports event in New York City has attracted so much attention around the world." Suddenly, everybody all over the world knew who the Cosmos were. American journalists like Tom Brokaw, Howard Cosell and others talked about that first game, and said soccer had finally arrived in the United States. Lamar Hunt, the owner of the opposing Dallas team in that first game, watched on TV from a motel room in Tyler, Texas. "As I watched," Hunt later recalled, "I thought, 'Well, we've made it. It was worth the agony, the lean years.'"

Indeed, the soccer boom was much bigger and more immediate than anyone—even the most daring dreamers, like Steve Ross or Clive Toye—could possibly have imagined. After that first game, the Cosmos embarked on trips to places that were supposedly soccer wastelands, cities like Los Angeles, Seattle and Vancouver, as well as more developed markets like Boston and Washington, D.C. No matter where we went, in every city we broke attendance records. In Boston, the crowd mobbed me after I scored a goal, and even tweaked my ankle a bit as they tried to wrest away my shoes for souvenirs. In Washington, D.C., some thirty-five thousand people turned out, the biggest NASL crowd ever. (A few nights later, for another game, only twenty-one hundred fans showed up.) Even in LA—where the team played in a tiny stadium at El Camino Junior College—the twelve-thousand-seat venue was filled to capacity. Everywhere we went, people were friendly, enthusiastic and surprisingly knowledgeable about soccer. It was as if America's soccer fans had just been waiting for a ray of light to signal that dawn had finally come for their sport.

The game also seemed to tap perfectly into the zeitgeist of the United States in the mid-1970s, as the Baby Boomers got older. Dick Berg, the general manager of the Dallas Tornadoes at the time, said: "Soccer is an antiestablishment game. It is not sanctified like the NFL or specialized like the NBA. Its individual play and constant movement are anticorporate, and we're attracting the young adults who grew up in the sixties, the people who were then anti-Vietnam, had longer hair and listened to different music. They spend dollars now, and soccer has attracted them."

Well, I don't know if all of that was true. But we certainly hit a nerve. Kids who played soccer at school started begging their parents to take them to our games. Even more important—in fact, this would prove to the most critical development of all—half the fans at NASL games were women. *Sports Illustrated* crowed: "Nobody in his proper mind would have dreamed that in a few short weeks, Pelé would be as well-known as Joe Namath," the quarterback for one of the teams in New York that played the "other" kind of football—the Jets.

I felt like half of my responsibilities were on the field as a player, and the rest were off the field as a kind of professor and ambassador of soccer. It was during those early weeks that I coined a phrase that would follow me around for the rest of my life. The American reporters were always asking me questions about "soccer." This word was strange to me at first, since I'd always known the sport—even in English—as "football." In order to distinguish between what I played and American football, which I found a bit dull and brutal and punctuated by too many pauses, I said that the sport I played was a *jogo bonito*—a "beautiful game." The phrase stuck, and has been used to describe soccer around the world ever since.

Those were some of the favorite days of my professional life. Was I as fast or as powerful as I had been ten years before? Goodness, no. Did we win every game? Not even close. But there was a newness to everything, a tingly feeling of discovery that I suppose I hadn't really felt since that first World Cup in Sweden in 1958. Every time we went to a new city, and people came out to greet us, it felt like we were planting our flag, the flag of soccer, never to retreat again.

Freed of the expectations and pressures of home—and also, I'm certain, more mature and comfortable in my own skin than when I was younger—I found new pleasures within soccer. I clowned around with my teammates, and generally enjoyed getting to see America. In Seattle, we stayed in a hotel where my room was about three stories above the harbor. The manager lent me a fishing rod and a bucket of salmon fillets for bait, and within seconds I hooked a small sand shark. I pulled it up to the balcony as my teammates, incredulous, cracked up with laughter. What to do with the shark? One of them ran into the room and came back with a table leg, which he used to bash the shark in the head. It wasn't quite like being back home, fishing in the Baurú River—a shark would have caused the whole town to flee in terror! But it was close enough.

We took our games very seriously, but everybody knew we had a larger purpose: promoting the game, and making soccer viable in the United States. And so there was a degree of camaraderie, even with the opposing team, that was sometimes harder to find in more advanced leagues. For example, I had a big problem with a particularly nefarious element of sports in the United States in the 1970s: Astroturf. Artificial surfaces in today's modern era could be easily mistaken for soft, lush, regular grass. But during those years, Astroturf surfaces were essentially concrete floors with a little strip of green rug on them. I'd rarely been exposed to them before, and I felt like my feet were on fire. Some players for the Seattle Sounders told me that Astroturf was easier if you just had plain tennis shoes on; when I said I didn't have any, one of them kindly lent me a pair. I was gratified, if a bit paranoid—in Brazil, or any other hypercompetitive league, an opposing player would have put rusty nails in the soles or something! (I'm exaggerating, but only a little bit.)

All the camaraderie, and the practice, brought us closer together. The Cosmos would finish the 1975 season with a losing record, and miss the playoffs. We still needed more talent. But we felt like we had laid the groundwork for something. And the off-season—well, that was going to be a lot of fun too.

12

I was a grown man, but I was also living outside my country for the first time in my life. So there were times when I, once again, felt like that fourteen-year-old kid on the bus from Baurú to Santos: unsure of myself, far from home, excited but somewhat lost. I missed Brazil. I missed the beaches, the steak asados on Sunday afternoons. Most of all, I missed the fans at places like Vila Belmiro, Pacaembu and the Maracanã. Sometimes, I'd just pick a star in the southern sky and stare at it, wondering what was going on back home, and what I was missing.

Luckily, I was able to bring some of the comforts of home with me to the United States. The biggest of all was family. Rose and the kids joined me, and we lived in a nice apartment on the East Side. Kely Cristina and Edinho picked up English quickly, like all kids do, and settled into their American school. My brother Zoca also joined us, working at Trenton University and giving soccer clinics for kids. My parents spent a lot of time with us, and it was funny—the Nascimento clan maybe spent even more time together in New York than we had in Santos.

Furthermore, New York wasn't the kind of place where you really had time to be homesick. Unusually for me, given the fact that I usually cared about few things but soccer, I really lost myself in all the cultural options the city offered. Almost every weekend, I went to some kind of show or event with Rose. Sometimes we went to Broadway musicals, but very often we went to the ballet. There was something about ballet that really spoke to me and reminded me of soccer—the combination of strength, fluidity of movement, and elegance. I'd sit, transfixed, for hours and hours, week after week. I loved Cirque du Soleil for the same reasons. Watching it, I felt like I understood—I felt I could anticipate many of the moves the performers made.

There were also less . . . wholesome . . . pursuits. Steve Ross' empire at Warner Communications opened up a new world of interesting people, including many singers and Hollywood stars who either lived in New York or were constantly passing through. One of the celebrities I saw most often was Rod Stewart, who was both a Warner Brothers artist and a huge soccer fan. Sometimes he visited the Cosmos facilities and kicked the ball around with us during practices. Rod would take me out to Studio 54, the famous—infamous?—restaurant and night-club that was the center of the Manhattan party scene in the 1970s. We'd sit there and listen to music and have a good time. A few times, Mick Jagger joined us. So did Liza Minnelli, Björn Borg and Andy Warhol—who proclaimed that I was the exception to his rule about everybody getting fifteen minutes of fame. "Pelé will be famous forever," he said, with a good bit of exaggeration.

Even in such company, I stuck by the "No drugs or alcohol" philosophy that I'd followed over the years. This vow had been enormously helpful in preserving my body, and allowing me to keep playing soccer at age thirty-five—and beyond. But it made me a bit unusual for the Studio 54 crowd. One night, Rod got a little frustrated with me and said: "Damn, Pelé! You don't drink, and you don't do drugs. So what *do* you do?"

Well, I had my weaknesses, particularly when it came to members of the opposite sex. And you can believe that there was no shortage of temptation in New York during the mid-1970s, especially as the Cosmos' fame began to blast off. I remember one visit to the Warner building, where the actor Robert Redford also had an office. We were both standing in the lobby, chatting, when a group of autograph seekers came running toward us. I saw Robert flinch in anticipation. Surprise slowly spread across his face when he realized the fans were coming not for him, but for me.

"Wow!" he said, marveling, standing there by himself as I signed away. "You *are* famous!"

Fame also helped me with something really important—impressing my kids. This was a task that became much more difficult over the years, as it does for all parents. When my daughter, Kely Cristina, was a teenager, she kept begging me to introduce her to the actor William Hurt, whom she had a huge crush on. So I took Kely to a cocktail party in New York for the launch of his movie *Kiss of the Spider Woman*. When we walked in, William saw me and screamed: "You're Pelé! You're Pelé!" He was practically shrieking. He threw himself on me and started literally kissing my feet. I laughed and laughed. Kely was impressed, maybe for the first and last time ever!

I hoped that coming to New York would help build a bridge to my post-soccer life, and I wasn't disappointed. Some great opportunities showed up on that front, too. I had already done some acting in Brazil, including a role in a *telenovela* back in the 1960s in which I played an alien scouting out earth for an invasion. I wasn't a very good actor (and I'm being kind), but it was great fun. One day over lunch in New York, the director Steven Spielberg proposed making a film of me playing soccer on the moon. To tell the truth, I never quite understood that idea—maybe he confused me with Marcos Cesar Pontes, another famous citizen of Baurú who became the first Brazilian in space! Eventually, I did appear in a big-time Hollywood movie: *Escape to Victory*, a film starring Sylvester Stallone and Michael Caine. I played a soccer player. This, you could say, was less of a stretch for me.

My contract with Warner included a bunch of cross-promotional deals. When they released a new video-gaming system for Atari, for example, I helped launch it. And there was also a whole network of people I met through Brazilians living in the United States. I had a business partner whom I helped open up some chiropractor clinics in Los Angeles. He, in turn, knew another Brazilian who was a professional cook for an up-and-coming pop star who, after years singing in an ensemble, was launching his solo career. And that was how I came to be invited to Michael Jackson's eighteenth birthday party in California. He was very quiet, very well dressed, and very polite. A simple young man, but obviously very delicate. I was saddened by what happened to him many years later.

Why do I mention all of this? All the contact with stars and celebrities—it was great fun. I was having the time of my life. But, looking back, there was also a constructive purpose: It helped make soccer glamorous. By giving the sport a little glitz, a little razzle-dazzle, we convinced many Americans that soccer must be worth watching. Celebrities started taking ownership of NASL teams—Mick Jagger took a stake in a team in Philadelphia, joined by fellow rockers Peter Frampton and Paul Simon. Elton John headlined the ownership group for the franchise in Los Angeles, the Aztecs. And, just as important, other big-name players around the world became excited about playing in the United States, too. My words had proven true after all: Soccer had indeed arrived.

13

After the Cosmos missed the playoffs in 1975, I told Steve Ross and Clive Toye that we'd need at least one more big-name player. "I can't do this alone," I said.

I felt bad saying this—I really liked my teammates—but there is no substitute for talent in professional sports, and the brutal truth was that we simply didn't have enough of it. Opposing teams were able to assign three or even four defenders to me, without my teammates making them pay for their decision. "We're not going to win this way," I said. "Please go look in South America or Europe for some other players who will join us."

I'll say this about Steve Ross—with him, you didn't need to ask twice. Before long, the Cosmos signed two more big-name stars of international soccer: the Italian forward Giorgio Chinaglia, and Franz Beckenbauer, the captain of the West German team that had just won the 1974 World Cup. These were dynamite acquisitions that solidified the NASL as a big-time league—and outraged many people in soccer's "Old World." Signing Chinaglia was such a coup that he "had to be smuggled out of Italy after the season started for fear of widespread rioting," one newspaper wrote, probably with some embellishment, but only a bit. When Beckenbauer arrived in New York, a huge crowd of people, including many kids, went to the airport to greet his plane. Beckenbauer later said coming to the United States was "the best decision I ever made."

When all the other clubs saw the stars the Cosmos were signing, they decided to follow suit. Eusébio da Silva Ferreira, the star of the Portuguese national team that had eliminated Brazil in 1966, signed with the Las Vegas Quicksilvers. The Tampa Bay club signed Tommy Smith, a sharp-tongued defender who had played many years for Liverpool. The legend George Best, of Northern Ireland, would soon sign with the Los Angeles Aztecs. There were also new expansion teams in places like San Diego and Tulsa, Oklahoma. The competition was on!

That 1976 season saw us make enormous progress on the field. Chinaglia led the league with nineteen goals and eleven assists, and helped take a lot of the focus away from me. I was able to get some more breathing room on the field, and in one game in Honolulu I scored four goals—including three in a fifteen-minute span in the second half. We played to packed houses almost everywhere we went, and the crowds in New York were so big that the owners moved the team over to Yankee Stadium. Winning helped fan the popular ardor even more: We finished the season with sixteen wins and eight losses.

We made the playoffs, and faced the Tampa Bay Rowdies. That team was a remarkable success story, in some ways the opposite of our New York club. They did have that one star: Tommy Smith. But where New York was glitz and glamour, Tampa Bay was small-town pluck and ingenuity. Players and coaches would show up at a restaurant after games to autograph T-shirts. The team's trademarked motto was "The Rowdies are a kick in the grass"—just a tiny bit racy for the United States back then! Before every game, a group of cheerleaders called "Wowdies" ran on the field and released balloons for their adoring fans. And then the whole crowd would sing along with the theme song: "The Rowdies run here, the Rowdies run there, they kick the ball around!" Yes, it was all a bit hokey, but people loved it—and the team was thriving. Even though it was an expansion team in 1975, Tampa

Bay won the NASL championship that year. And they looked like they might just pull it off again in 1976.

The fans in Tampa Bay were knowledgeable, and very kind. Before the game started, as I took the field, the crowd gave me a standing ovation. It was a marvelous display of sportsmanship. Too bad it was the highlight of the game for me!

The game started well enough. But the Tampa Bay team played exceptional defense, and I couldn't get free of my man to save my life. On one play, I got knocked down, and as I lay there on the ground, with Tommy Smith standing over me, the Rowdies scored yet another goal to put the game away.

We were disappointed by the loss, to be sure. But I was happy that the level of competition was up, and the NASL felt like a real league now. Nearly thirty-seven thousand people turned out for our game against Tampa—a very good crowd for any American sport. "Soccer Is Getting a Toehold," *Sports Illustrated* proclaimed in August 1976. None of us suspected that, in some ways, the opposite was true. Storm clouds were gathering that would soon threaten everything we had worked so hard to build.

14

One of my greatest pleasures in New York City was to wander into Central Park by myself, and try to find a group of kids playing soccer. This required a little bit of hunting in the early days—it was much easier to find people throwing a baseball or an American football in one of the park's huge, green meadows. But eventually, with some persistence, I'd come across a group kicking around a little black and white ball, and I'd smile.

I'd just watch them at first, my arms folded, maybe standing in the shade of a tree. I wouldn't say anything. Inevitably, someone would see me standing there. You can imagine the surprise! And then I'd go talk to them for a while, show them a few moves, and maybe give them tips. This was an era when Polaroid instant cameras really became all the rage, and somebody always seemed to have one handy. I'd pose with the group, all of us giving the Brazilian-style thumbs-up sign. And then I'd shake their hands or hug them good-bye, and disappear back into the urban jungle.

It made me so happy to spread my love for soccer to new people. I was able to do this in more formal ways, as well. In the early 1970s, I signed a

243

contract with PepsiCo to do a series of soccer workshops for kids around the world called the International Youth Football Program. Professor Mazzei and I collaborated together for this project, and we traveled to sixty-four countries, giving workshops to kids on how to play soccer better. The idea was a total triumph—it cost nothing for coaches, schools or players. For me, it was a great example of what corporations could do to make the world a better place, while also promoting their product.

Also working with PepsiCo, we produced a book and a coaching movie called *Pelé: The Master and His Method*, which thankfully has survived for posterity and continues to be watched by some young people today. In the movie, we broke down the "beautiful game" into its most basic elements: ball control, juggling, dribbling, passing, trapping, heading and—finally—shooting ("The not so gentle art of scoring goals," as we called it). I demonstrated each skill. I wore special shoes with lighter-color patches on the parts of the foot that are best used for shooting—a lot of kids mistakenly thought that they could kick the ball with the most speed and accuracy using the front of their foot, when the side is usually much better.

We worked really hard to produce a film that not only showed the game's technical skills, but transmitted some of soccer's romance as well. During one scene, the camera zoomed in on a soccer ball, and the narrator said: "Fifteen ounces of leather and compressed air . . . a dead object? No, not really. Just resting. Waiting for a signal from its master." Then I started to kick the ball around a bit, juggling it on my shoes and knees, and the narrator continued talking. "And suddenly it's full of life. Doing everything that Pelé wants it to."

Those drills were the easy part. The bigger challenge was how to transmit to kids the importance and fundamentals of true team play— which of course had become a particular obsession of mine since 1970. So we filmed many of the scenes back at the old Vila Belmiro field in Santos, with some of my old teammates. We also filmed on a little village field, and on the beach, where we asked some kids to try their luck at a Pelé-style bicycle kick. In one scene, I tied a ball to a tree branch with a rope and headed it over and over—just like Dondinho had taught me so many years before.

"But even for Pelé, there was a time when the ball didn't always obey him," the narrator said. "It was only hours of lonely practice as a boy that gave him this skill. Often he had no real soccer ball to practice with. He had to make do with whatever he could, maybe a ball of old rags tied with string . . ." Well, you know all that by now.

Here, again, the moment in history we were living in helped our efforts a lot. New technology—the home film projector and, soon, the VCR—meant that more kids than ever were able to watch movies like this in their own homes. Just a few years before, that would have been unthinkable—if you wanted to watch a movie, you either had to go to the cinema or hope they showed it on one of the handful of TV channels available. Meanwhile, the decision to do the movie in English—despite the fact that mine was still a work in progress—was also a huge boost. This was the era when, thanks to American business and the spread of TV and other communications, you could suddenly find English speakers not just in the United States or England, but in places like Eastern Europe and South Asia as well. They, too, were able to see and appreciate the movie, making it even more popular. Once again, we were in the right place at the right time as the world was changing.

Each of these projects helped, in their small way, to spread the gospel of soccer. Sure enough, as time passed, I'd go for my walks in Central Park and it became much easier to find kids playing soccer (and much harder to sneak up on them!). But as it turned out, the biggest triumph of the sport wasn't really playing out in New York, or Boston, or any other big cities. The truly extraordinary growth occurred instead in places like Plano, Texas; Prince George's County, Maryland; or Grosse Pointe, Michigan. Soccer turned out to be tailor-made for the more spacious, suburban United States that blossomed during the seventies and eighties. After all, there was never any shortage of space to build new soccer fields, and the sport held great appeal for boys and girls alike, eager to participate in a sport that perfectly represented the American spirit of equality and fair play. All of my doubts about the game's future melted away. In the end, it turned out that soccer and the United States were made for each other.

15

Just as Santos once had, the Cosmos of Pelé toured the world—playing games in seemingly every corner of the world, from China to India to Venezuela to France. One of my favorite memories is of a trip to that beloved old stomping ground: Sweden. We returned to Gothenburg for a match against a local team, which we won 3–1. But the biggest surprise of all was at the team hotel, when an attractive blond woman approached me.

"Do you know who I am?" she said earnestly.

I'm embarrassed to admit that I didn't, not at first. But when she introduced herself by name, I remembered instantly: It was Ilena, the Swedish girl I'd met some twenty years before, way back in 1958. She had brought along her young daughter, who was her carbon copy—blond and beautiful.

I gave Ilena a huge hug. She had read about my visit in a local newspaper, and wanted to see me. We talked for the longest time about that magical summer, and everything that had happened in the years since. It felt so good to reconnect with someone whose life had intersected with mine so many years before, but whom I'd lost touch with because of distance and time. Plus, now I actually spoke some English, so I could understand much more of what she was saying!

"I always knew you'd do well," Ilena said, smiling. "Soccer has been very good to you, hasn't it?"

16

The 1977 season was my final one with the Cosmos, and really the most fabulous farewell from professional soccer that a guy could possibly ask for. The team moved once again—to the brand-new Giants Stadium just outside New York, where we could play before even greater crowds. Attendance nearly doubled once more, and we pulled an average of thirty-four thousand people to our games that year. The crowds were frantic, studded by celebrities, and increasingly knowledgeable about the game—no more cheering for errant shots from twenty yards out! That was also the year that the Cosmos signed my old friend Carlos Alberto—my Santos teammate and the defender who scored that final goal against Italy in the 1970 Cup. I was surrounded by friends and great players, we were playing excellent soccer, and I was living in one of the greatest cities in the world. I felt like I was in paradise.

That final season also saw the Cosmos play for the first time in the so-called Soccer Bowl—the NASL's championship game. As you can tell by the name, the NASL had borrowed some elements from American football, including a tradition of playing the championship game on a neutral site. In Portland, Oregon, we played Soccer Bowl III against the Seattle Sounders in front of some thirty-five thousand people. Before the game, all of my teammates came up to me and said they wanted to send me out with one last championship. I was deeply touched. And sure enough, thanks to goals by Stephen Hunt and Chinaglia—the Italian forward that Steve Ross had acquired—the Cosmos won its first Soccer Bowl!

A few weeks later, on October 1, 1977, the Cosmos staged a "farewell" game for me. I had played one hundred and eleven games for Cosmos, scoring sixty-five goals. Of course, it wasn't the first "farewell" I'd played in, by any means. But if anybody rolled their eyes, they were polite enough to do so in private. Friends and former rivals from Brazil and all over the world came to New York to watch the game. The best part of all was the opponent—the Cosmos were going to play Santos.

There wasn't a hotter ticket in New York that day. Every single seat in Giants stadium was full, and we had some eighty thousand people show up. More than six hundred fifty journalists from thirty-eight nations also attended. President Jimmy Carter gave a speech, and Muhammad Ali came and saw me in the locker room. In classic Ali style, he said of me: "I don't know if he's a good player, but I'm definitely prettier than him."

Before the game started, we made one last gesture toward the growing popularity of the game in the States. Nine youth teams formed a circle around the middle of the field—six of them boys' teams, two of them girls' teams, and one team made up of athletes from the Special Olympics. They dribbled some balls around to show off their considerable skills. Then the captains from the last several winning teams of the World Cup walked out on the field together: Hilderaldo Bellini, my captain when Brazil won in 1958; Bobby Moore, England's captain in 1966; Carlos Alberto, our 1970 captain; and my New York Cosmos teammate Franz Beckenbauer, captain of West Germany's winning side in 1974.

I was honored that so many good friends made the trip. But there was an even bigger surprise visitor at that game: Dondinho, my dad.

After so many years of soccer, he had come to only a precious few of my games. He always supported me, of course, but he didn't like to travel and he preferred to keep his distance from the mad crowds at the stadiums. On this most special of days, the true and final farewell of my long career, Dondinho made the effort to come. The sight of the man who had taught me everything I knew about soccer, walking out there on the field of Giants Stadium that day, was one of the most profoundly emotional moments I ever had.

As you might guess, I was crying before the game even started! I scored a goal in the first half, and then at halftime, I switched jerseys—and, in a gesture toward my past, I played the second half for Santos. Unfortunately I didn't score any goals for Santos, but nobody really seemed to care. When it was over, they supplied me with a microphone and I gave a short speech to the crowd and all my teammates, which I ended by shouting: "Love! Love! Love!" It might not have been the most eloquent conclusion, but I was overwhelmed with emotion and it reflected what was in my heart. Then I grabbed both a Brazilian and a U.S. flag and paraded them around the field, riding on the shoulders of my teammates.

It was three weeks before my thirty-seventh birthday. I was now financially secure, an icon in the United States, and truly happy with my life. I was now done playing for good, and what Waldemar de Brito had once predicted was true: I had my whole life in front of me.

17

For a fleeting moment, it looked like all that effort might have been for naught—suddenly and violently washed away, like budding leaves by a spring rainstorm.

The Cosmos and the NASL, despite all their success, had made some grave mistakes. They had expanded far too fast, for one thing, with a league of twenty-four teams by 1980. Worse, the spending spree on international players, as every team in the league tried to sign their own version of Pelé, backfired in several different ways. Teams ended up signing a bunch of name-brand players who were washed up by the time they got to the NASL: The league began acquiring a reputation in Europe and elsewhere as an "elephants' graveyard," with poor quality of play. The emphasis on foreign talent also took roster spots away from American players who could have, in turn, better connected with local fans and—crucially—helped produce the next generation of soccer stars in the United States.

Worst of all, all that spending on foreign stars proved to be awfully expensive. In 1977, my final year in the league, only two teams turned a profit: Minnesota and Seattle. That's right: Even the Cosmos, the team with by far the league's most robust attendance and international name recognition, was operating in the red.

The league held on for a while, and thrived for a few years after I left. The Cosmos' peak attendance for a single year was actually in 1979, when they drew an average of 46,700 fans a game to Giants Stadium. But the rest of the league was struggling as the hype slowly faded away. Before long, only half the league's teams were averaging better than ten thousand fans a game. In 1985, the NASL collapsed—taking the Cosmos with them.

All these developments left me heartbroken. I worried in the late 1980s that soccer in the United States was "dying," as I told reporters at the time. But I should have had more faith in the game. After all, the financial failures of one group of businessmen couldn't erase all the hard work we had done. They couldn't erase the appeal of a beautiful game that had several years to take root in very fertile soil.

As was highlighted in *Once in a Lifetime*, a fine documentary film released in 2007 about the Cosmos' rise and fall, the popularity of our team endured. It echoed through time in unpredictable, but very fulfilling ways. For example: I've mentioned that, when the Cosmos signed Franz Beckenbauer, a group of children mobbed him at the airport upon his arrival in New York. One of the kids present at the airport that day was Mike Windischmann. Mike was a ball boy from the Cosmos starting in 1975, the year that I signed with the club. Well, when Mike grew up, he became an excellent player in his own right, and was named the captain of the United States national soccer team! He even led the U.S. team into the 1990 World Cup. This, of course, was the first time the Americans had qualified since 1950, when they famously upset the English team on Brazilian soil, as I've mentioned.

Indeed, the generation that came of age during the 1970s—during the Cosmos years—changed everything. Even if the NASL disappeared, and American professional soccer went into a kind of hibernation in the 1980s, the love for soccer they had acquired did not.

Even during the darkest moments, soccer was still being played on thousands of big, grassy fields throughout America. I'm flattered to say that some people even referred to the American kids who grew up playing soccer in the 1970s and 1980s as "the children of Pelé." Mia Hamm, the greatest women's soccer player ever in the United States, if not the world, spoke of how she used to attend our games religiously when the Cosmos played in Washington, D.C. Major League Soccer, the league that blossomed in the United States and thrived in ways the original NASL hadn't, thanks in part to much more prudent financial management, remains full of players who were touched in some ways by what we did. Jay Heaps, a former star player and now the coach of the New England Revolution, was born the year after I arrived in New York. But he still said that he watched *Pelé: The Master and His Method* over and over again on his VCR as a kid. He said he even tied a soccer ball to a tree branch and bounced it on his head for hours on end to practice headers! It tickles me to no end that, even today, Dondinho's techniques are still influencing soccer players, sixty years later and five thousand long miles away from Baurú.

The real coup, the one that secured the future of soccer in the United States for good, came in 1988. Several countries were competing for the right to host the 1994 World Cup. One of the finalists was the United States. I had dreamed since the 1970s of getting a World Cup on American soil—I thought, once again, that the exposure to top-shelf talent was necessary to seduce the discriminating U.S. public and win them over to the game. If we could gather the world's best players in their prime and have them play in stadiums all over the United States, it would be even more effective than the Cosmos had been in its heyday.

My zeal for an American World Cup had a hitch—the other two finalists to host the 1994 Cup were Morocco and . . . Brazil. You can imagine the rage back home when I publicly supported the United States' bid. Lots of sports columnists and others in Brazil accused me of being a stooge for corporate America, or just unpatriotic. I had my reasons, though.

First, I believed that we had a limited window of time to ensure soccer's future in the world's richest country: We needed a "big bang" of quality soccer to get everybody's attention, and hopefully lead to a revival of a professional American league. Second, I believed that the

Brazil of that era was in no condition to host a World Cup. I was relieved that democracy had returned in 1985, but unfortunately the transition out of the dictatorship had been chaotic in many ways. Brazil's financial situation—always difficult—had never been worse. Poverty was soaring. So was inflation, as the newly elected government spent far more money than it took in. Remember how upset people were when, in the early 1960s, prices in Brazil were doubling every year? Now, in the late 1980s, they were doubling every *month*. Who in their right mind thought we could afford to build a bunch of new stadiums, or even renovate existing ones, in a situation such as that? As I said publicly at the time: "A country where millions of people are starving and which has the Third World's largest foreign debt cannot consider the sponsorship of a World Cup with government money." This was an extremely unpopular thing for me to say, but it was the truth.

On July 4, 1988—Independence Day in the United States—FIFA announced that the United States had won the right to host the World Cup tournament in 1994. I was proud to have done my part, and gleefully told reporters that the decision was "a dream come true." Alan Rothenberg, then the head of the U.S. Soccer Federation, thanked me for my help and later said: "Pelé was the single most important person in bringing the World Cup to the U.S.A."

18

When the shining moment finally came, the American World Cup was a bigger success than even I had imagined. The average attendance of nearly sixty-nine thousand fans per game shattered the previous World Cup record of fifty-one thousand, which had been set in England in 1966. The U.S. team played well enough to make it out of group play to the elimination round, but they were unlucky enough to draw a very difficult opponent in the Round of Sixteen: Brazil.

This matchup—which also occurred on the Fourth of July, oddly enough—sparked a huge media firestorm as pundits breathlessly asked: Which team will Pelé support? The tension was made worse by the very long title drought—twenty-four years—which, combined with all the problems Brazil was suffering in the mid-1990s, had the whole country on edge. "Anxiety has broken out like a national rash," the *New York Times* wrote. "It's not because the Brazilians are afraid of the Americans. It is just that, in Brazil, there are only two results: stylish victory and panic."

That still makes me laugh, mostly because it was—and is—so true! But in the end, there was no reason for nerves of any kind. Obviously, I supported my home country, while also hoping for a good performance from the country that had treated me with such marvelous generosity.

The final result was perfect: a very closely fought 1–0 victory for Brazil, played before eighty-four thousand raucous, flag-waving fans at Stanford Stadium in northern California. The United States' defense was incredible that day, allowing only a goal to Bebeto in the seventy-fourth minute. The result was in doubt until the final whistle blew. Even if the Americans didn't win, they got to see international soccer at its absolute finest. The U.S. national team would build on that performance, and do even better in ensuing World Cups.

As for Brazil, that 1994 team was a very, very good one. My old teammate and coach from 1970, Zagallo, was now back in the fold, serving as the top assistant for the team manager: Carlos Alberto Parreira. We had an amazing crop of players including Dunga, Bebeto, Romário, and a phenomenal young talent named Ronaldo—who was seventeen, the same age I had been in Sweden in 1958. Although Ronaldo didn't play much in 1994, he would eventually go on to break not only my Brazilian mark for most career goals scored in World Cups, but the world record as well, with fifteen.

Speaking of Sweden, they also had an outstanding team that year, and they were our opponents in the semifinals. That was a toughly fought game, and it almost seemed like the Swedes would get revenge for that day so long ago in Stockholm—until Brazil finally got a goal in the eightieth minute from Romário, and held on to win 1–0 to advance to the championship game.

In the final, Italy played a very spirited match, just like they always did against us. Regular time ended in a scoreless draw—and so did overtime. That was the first World Cup final ever to be decided by penalties, which was a bit of a shame. But nobody seemed to mind—least of all the Brazilians, who ended up winning.

The crowd erupted in cheers. The U.S. vice president, Al Gore, came down to the field to present the trophy to Dunga. I was there on the field, too, overcome with pride in my adopted country, and my favorite sport. Both of them, despite long odds, had conquered the hearts of everyone.

BRAZIL, 2014

1

'm often asked: "Was there ever a time in your career when you choked? When you buckled under pressure on the soccer field?"

Oh yes, I say. Big-time. But it was also the moment that, in turn, opened up one of the most rewarding chapters of my life.

In 1969, the year before the World Cup in Mexico, I began to approach an unprecedented milestone in soccer—one thousand career goals. This was considered a particularly difficult achievement, in part because of the sheer number of games I needed to play to get there. My career totals included my games with Santos, the Brazilian team, and even the year I played with the military upon my return from Sweden. After winning the World Cup, I, like all other Brazilian youths during the 1950s, had to perform a year of military service when I turned eighteen. I thought it was a great message, that everybody was treated equally—and the military got some benefits out of the arrangement too, including a pretty good forward for their in-house team!

It was a lot of soccer, a lot of sweat and hard work. As I've already said, Santos scheduled an extraordinary amount of games, hoping to cash in as much as they could on our popularity. In 1969, for example,

I played nine games in March, six in April and six in May. In June, Santos had games against Corinthians, São Paulo FC and Palmeiras— the three powerhouse teams of São Paulo. I also played for Brazil against England, the defending world champions, in a tough 1–0 victory. Finally, at the end of the month, I traveled with Santos to Milan, Italy, to play a powerful Inter team. And that was a relatively easy month, with only five games! Some people, then as now, tried to downplay the significance of the one-thousand-goal milestone, saying it was inflated by all those games. To which I respond: I certainly wasn't in charge of our schedule. And I think I should get *some* credit for not simply collapsing in exhaustion on the field!

In any case, most people thought it was a number worth celebrating. "One thousand goals in soccer is comparatively a greater feat than that of Babe Ruth's 714 lifetime home runs in baseball," the Associated Press wrote at the time. The Brazilian poet Carlos Drummond de Andrade was particularly kind, declaring: "The difficulty, the extraordinary thing, is not to score one thousand goals, like Pelé. It is to score one goal like Pelé."

The only problem with having people say such nice things is that, afterward, you have to live up to what they say. And by October 1969, as I cleared the nine-hundred-ninety-goal threshold, I was feeling physically tired, and more than a bit rattled emotionally as well. I didn't like all the pressure being focused solely on me—it was the same kind of uncharacteristically nervous reaction I'd experience during my "farewell" games some years later. Nobody really cared about my nerves, though, nor should they have. I was a professional, doing what I loved. The contingent of fans and reporters from all over the world grew and grew with each passing day. Before our road games, teams would stage parades, hang flags and even invite marching bands to honor me— even though I was playing for the opposing team!

Under the weight of all these expectations, I hit a wall. I couldn't score a goal to save my life. One of our games during that stretch ended in a 0–0 tie. During a match in Salvador, against Bahia, I had one shot bounce off the goalpost, and in a separate but equally agonizing near miss, I had the ball stolen from me at the goal line by a defender.

Things got so bad that Santos even decided to make me the goalie during a game against a small team in João Pessoa, in Brazil's northeast. This in itself wasn't a huge stretch for me: I had been the reserve goalie for Santos for many years, thanks to all that time practicing the position when I was a kid back in Baurú. But in this particular case, I think the club's leadership was probably just showing mercy on me.

With me seemingly stuck on 999 goals for eternity, Santos was due to play Vasco at the Maracanã, of all places. I played some big games in that stadium in my life, but I can't remember one quite as intense as that match. The date was the nineteenth of November, which is Brazil's Flag Day. The stadium was packed to capacity. There was a military marching band on the field, and a release of balloons into the sky. I felt like I was going to throw up.

Finally, a crossing pass came toward me, nice and high, just as I liked it. I was in perfect position to head the ball into the goal. I jumped as high as I could, kept my eyes open just like Dondinho had taught me, and . . .

Gooooalllllllllllll!

But wait—I hadn't touched the ball. Rene, a defender for Vasco, had jumped into the air to block me and ended up knocking it in himself—an own goal! I couldn't believe it! My God, I thought I'd never score again!

A few minutes later, though, as I was running into the penalty box with the ball, I was tripped up. The referee blew his whistle. A penalty kick! I couldn't believe it. This was how the one thousandth goal would happen?

Yes. I took a good long time to line up the shot, and even realized that I was trembling a bit. But when the moment came, I ran up to the ball, made a little pause to fool the goalkeeper, and then knocked it in.

This time, for real:

Goaaaaaaalllllllllllllllllllllll!!!!!!!!!!!!!

The crowd roared. I ran into the back of the net, picked up the ball, and kissed it. The stadium erupted with firecrackers and cheers. A phalanx of reporters ran over to me with microphones and TV cameras and asked me how I felt. I hadn't really thought about what to say beforehand, so in the heat of the moment, I spoke my mind—and I dedicated the goal to the children of Brazil. "We need to look after the little kids," I said. "That's what we need to be worrying about."

Why did I say this? A few months earlier, I had left a training session in Santos a little early and I saw a group of kids, maybe twelve or thirteen years old, the kind that in Brazil you give a few coins to "keep an eye on your car." It's really common, and always a bit of a shakedown, to tell the truth. In this case, the kids weren't even making any pretenses about watching anything because I caught them trying to steal a car that was parked near mine. I asked them what they were doing. They ignored me at first, until they realized who I was and then they perked up a bit. "Don't worry, Pelé," one of them assured me. "We'll only steal cars from São Paulo." I laughed in shock and informed them they wouldn't be stealing any cars at all!

They smirked and scattered after that. But the incident stuck with me, and it worried me a lot. I too had engaged in my share of childhood high jinks—recall the peanuts on the train that ended up as seed capital for the Sete de Setembro team back in Baurú. But it seemed like life for Brazilian children was becoming so much more brutal, so much more dangerous, even if the economy was growing a lot in those years. Brazil had been transformed from a mostly rural country to an overwhelmingly urban one in just a generation. A lot of the community bonds I remembered from Baurú, where everybody knew everybody else, had been destroyed as neighborhoods broke up and people moved to the big cities. Instead of swimming in rivers and snatching mangoes from neighbors' trees, as my generation had, many youths were now trapped inside giant walled apartment blocks and experimenting with drugs. It seemed, to me anyway, like there was a huge difference between stealing peanuts and stealing cars. And of course having kids of my own made these concerns more personal than ever.

Well, it's funny, the way life works: My comment about the kids ended up being far more memorable and important than anything else that happened that day, including the one thousandth goal or my struggles to score it.

At the time, I endured a lot of criticism from people in the media who said I was being a demagogue, or insincere. But I thought it was important to use that moment, with the whole world watching, to draw attention to a critical matter beyond the soccer field, to a social issue that had begun to worry me greatly. As I got older, I was beginning to realize that sport could—and should—have a larger purpose, beyond just goals, passes and championships. As it turned out, despite all the cynicism and doubts, people in Brazil and around the world were actually listening to what I had to say.

2

was at a cocktail party in New York, during the Cosmos years, when a very elegant older woman was introduced to me.

"It's a pleasure to meet you, Pelé," she said. "I'm Eunice Kennedy Shriver."

I had met Mrs. Shriver's brother, President John F. Kennedy, some years before. I found him very charismatic and kind, and I was saddened by his death in 1963. But until that moment I knew very little about the rest of the family and the work they did. So I was very curious when Mrs. Shriver began speaking to me, that very night, about the program she had started a few years before, in 1968, to encourage athletics and sport among disabled people.

"We call it the Special Olympics," she told me. "And we would be honored if you would help us promote it."

I immediately accepted. I had never heard of a more worthy project. Over the years, I probably became closer to Mrs. Shriver than any other person in the United States, as I did my part to help promote the Special Olympics by appearing at events and meeting with the athletes. Mrs. Shriver was always very good to me—very serious, very astute.

She said she loved the happiness of the Brazilian people, our music and our dance. But she was focused above all on making the Special Olympics into a success. What began as a track meet in Chicago in 1968, with just fifteen hundred athletes, was transformed by 1983 into a mega-event with one million athletes from fifty countries. Playing a small part in that growth was one of the most gratifying experiences of my life. I'll never forget her timeless words: "In the Special Olympics, it is not the strongest body or the most dazzling mind that counts. It is the invincible spirit which overcomes all handicaps."

I was astounded by the American ability to promote charity, business and sport at the same time. I had never seen anything like it in Brazil. Mrs. Shriver was particularly skilled at organizing these events where people could get together to do good deeds, have fun and make money. One example was when a huge group of us gathered for a three-day weekend in Washington, D.C., to raise funds for the Special Olympics and also promote a new movie: *Superman*, the one starring Christopher Reeve.

A whole bunch of famous people were there, from Steve Ross to the American journalist Barbara Walters to Henry Kissinger (of course). Mrs. Shriver's daughter Maria, who was twenty-three, brought her boyfriend, an Austrian bodybuilder named Arnold Schwarzenegger. He was a lot quieter back then—his English was better than mine, but not by much. I asked him if he had played soccer back in Europe. "I prefer lifting weights," he said, smiling. "I'm better at it."

For the viewing of the *Superman* movie, President Carter and his wife were in attendance. Kissinger warmed up the crowd, talking about his past as a goalie back in Germany. "I want to thank you for coming to a movie that is dedicated to my life," he joked. And then, just before the feature started, the crowd saw a short film on the Special Olympics. I remember the room went totally quiet as all those kids talked about how important it was for them to have an athletic outlet of their own.

This, apart from being heart-warming, important work, was a tremendous learning experience for me. Charity and good work could be fun. It could be done effectively, with an eye toward specific, concrete results. Armed with this knowledge, I returned to Brazil, determined to do as much good as I possibly could back home.

3

B y the early 1990s, it seemed like things in Brazil couldn't get any worse. Yet somehow, they did. In addition to all our usual economic problems, we were hit by a series of almost unthinkable tragedies that were so terrible that the whole world wept with us. In 1992, a riot broke out at the Carandiru Penitentiary in São Paulo. Military police stormed the jail and opened fire: One hundred and eleven prisoners were killed. Just a few months later, in 1993, a group of gunmen opened fire on several dozen homeless children who were sleeping outside the Candelária Church in Rio de Janeiro. Eight of the kids, including some as young as eleven, were killed. The murderers, in that case, turned out to be policemen who apparently were angry over crime in downtown Rio and believed these helpless children should be punished for it.

The Candelária massacre, as it came to be known, was devastating for me and many Brazilians. I cried for days. It seemed to me like the culmination of all my fears about children in our country, the worries that I'd expressed back in 1969. It was proof that we lived in a profoundly sick society, one that had turned its back on its neediest and most vulnerable people.

The Brazil of my youth, the country of very rich and very poor people, hadn't changed much over the years, at least not in that respect. The gap between the social classes was as big as ever, and Brazil remained one of the most unequal countries in the world. Meanwhile, our national population had grown at an astonishing speed: from about sixty million people in 1956—the year I left Baurú on the bus for Santos—to one hundred seventy million or so people in 1990. Almost all of the growth had occurred in cities; the rural country of my youth was now, shockingly, eighty percent urban. Our cities were colossal, but jobs were few and far between. Many people lived short, violent lives in the *favelas* on hills above Rio and São Paulo. Few of us believed we would ever see things improve.

In 1994, just as the World Cup in the United States was going on, there was also a presidential campaign under way. I didn't pay much attention. As much as I dislike cynicism, I was convinced that politics would always be part of the problem in Brazil, not part of the solution. My history had certainly taught me to believe that.

The victor was a little different from previous Brazilian presidents, though. He was a famous sociologist from São Paulo named Fernando Henrique Cardoso. He had studied poverty and its causes up close, and he had performed studies back in the 1950s showing how black Brazilians had suffered from a lack of economic opportunities. Fernando Henrique, as people called him, was a leftist during the dictatorship, and had even gone into exile in Chile and France. But he had evolved over time and now wanted to make Brazil a modern country with a vibrant, integrated economy. He wasn't a charismatic guy, and while he spoke French, Spanish and English fluently, he sometimes struggled to speak in a language everyday Brazilians could understand. But, as the finance minister in the previous government, he had somehow managed to tame that old Brazilian problem of inflation. Prices rose a stunning twenty-five hundred percent in 1993, the worst year we ever had. But by the middle of 1994 they were barely going up at all. This unexpected success led him to run for president.

Fernando Henrique wasn't above using soccer to help his political agenda. In that respect, at least, I guess he was pretty similar to some of his predecessors. On July 1, 1994, three days before the World Cup game in California between Brazil and the United States, Fernando Henrique launched a new currency, called the *"real."* He hoped it would help stabilize prices even further. Of course, soccer would have no direct impact on whether a new currency succeeded or not. But, as Fernando Henrique later said, he did think that Brazilians might be more likely to accept the *real* if they were in a good mood and feeling confident about their country. What better way to accomplish that than by winning the World Cup?

So Fernando Henrique decided to stake his fate to that of the national team, inviting journalists and others to his apartment to watch as he sat in front of his television and cheered on Brazil. This was kind of a risky bet—after all, Brazil hadn't won a World Cup in twenty-four years! But, of course, everything worked out, and Brazil beat Italy in the championship that day at the Rose Bowl. Coincidence or not, the *real*'s launch was also a success. Fernando Henrique won the election in a landslide a few weeks later. Politics and soccer—together once again in Brazil. I couldn't believe it.

Sometime before the inauguration, in late 1994, I was invited to a meeting with Fernando Henrique in Brasilia. I didn't really know what to expect. He was very polite, and more down-to-earth than I'd expected. "One of the things we want to do is get more kids into school," Fernando Henrique said. "We think this, over time, will solve a lot of Brazil's problems."

This sounded great, but I didn't really see what it had to do with me, until he got to the point. "Pelé," he said, "I would like for you to be the extraordinary minister of sports in my government."

Oh, this was not a new idea. I was flattered, of course. But I had been offered the post by three previous presidents already in the past ten years, and I had declined. I told Fernando Henrique as much, politely thanked him, and prepared to leave.

"Well, I understand," he said softly. "But what about that appeal you made with your one thousandth goal, for the children of Brazil?"

Fernando Henrique said he wanted to make sports a fundamental part of his plan to coax kids into school. "This would be an opportunity for you to do something concrete, something real, to help the kids. So come on, Pelé. What do you think?"

I remember thinking: Man, this guy is good! Maybe it *was* time for me to stop talking about Brazilian politics, and actually do something to make a positive difference. Almost despite myself, I found myself saying "yes" to Fernando Henrique's offer. After so many years complaining about politics, now I was going to be part of the system.

4

've always been a very relaxed, informal guy, even by the standards of
Brazil—a country where people are, let's say, not known for wearing
suits and ties everywhere. So the pomp and decorum of Brasilia, our
capital, came as a shock at first. It was a city of elaborate titles, dark
suits, black sedans, and speeches where you had to acknowledge everybody important in a room by name before you were allowed to say a
single thing of substance! My friends didn't even know what to call me
anymore. Minister Edson? Minister Pelé? I'd had all kinds of nicknames over the years, including some that lightheartedly referenced my
race, like *negão* and *crioulo*. People I'd known for decades would come
up to me during those first few months at the ministry and say:

"Hey there, *crioulo*, what's up?"

And then they'd turn pale and say:

"Oops, sorry, Minister Edson . . ."

I'd just laugh and tell them: "No, no, relax. . . ."

It was all a new experience for me, but I was very proud of my new
position. I was honored to serve my country in an official capacity, and
thankful for the trust that the president and my fellow Brazilians had

placed in me. I was also proud to be the first black cabinet minister in the history of Brazil. That nearly two centuries passed after Brazil's independence for this to happen showed, once again, how much Afro-Brazilians had struggled to find opportunities. I was glad to help knock down that barrier, so that many more people could follow in my footsteps, which others soon did.

I did discover, to both my surprise and delight, that one could do quite a few good things from Brasilia. As Fernando Henrique had promised, our biggest focus was on convincing families to send their kids to school. This would address several of Brazil's most pressing problems, including, hopefully, the biggest of all: poverty. A 1992 study showed that fifteen percent of Brazilian children under the age of five showed signs of malnutrition. Obviously, this had horrible consequences for not only the present, but the future of Brazil as well. All told, about thirty-two million kids across the country lived in poverty—a number greater than the entire population of Canada. We believed that, if we could get kids into school and keep them there, we could ensure in the short term that they were eating better, and we could also keep them away from bad influences on the street that often led to crime. In the longer term, we would give them an education—which was clearly a necessary step to pull people out of poverty.

One of Fernando Henrique's ideas was a program called *bolsa escola*, which paid families a small cash stipend of a few hundred dollars every month as long as they kept their kids in school. This was very important—in fact, it would mark a turning point in Brazilian education, and the lives of many poor people as well. But I knew from my own experience that the kids themselves also needed a sweetener—they needed more excuses to go to school. After all, if there had been soccer at school back in Baurú, I might have skipped class a little less often as a kid!

So, with the help of many dedicated people at the sports ministry and elsewhere, we started a program that put low-cost sports facilities, like soccer fields and basketball courts, in many of our poorest neighborhoods. We called these facilities *vilas olimpicas,* or "Olympic villages." The name helped give them a big-time feel, but the *vilas* usually had a cost of well under a million dollars each. Since the Brazilian government was still very short of funds in those days, we were able to obtain much of the money from private sources like Xerox, an American company. Kids could use the *vilas* whenever they wanted, but— here was the key—they needed to prove they had been attending classes regularly if they wanted to get in. This requirement had two benefits: It gave kids an extra reason to attend class, and it also kept them off the streets after school, away from drugs and other problems, even if for just a few hours.

It was a simple idea, but man, was it effective. In many of the neighborhoods where we installed the *vilas*, school attendance soared, while youth crime dropped, in some cases to near zero. In 1997, U.S. President Bill Clinton and his wife, Hillary, came to Rio and visited a particularly successful *vila olimpica* in Mangueira, a poor neighborhood. President Clinton gave a speech in which he lauded the success of the program, and congratulated one of the students in Mangueira for being the first person in her family to go to university.

Afterward, President Clinton and I walked over to the soccer field. "Take it easy on me," he said, laughing. I smiled, and the press laughed and snapped lots of photos while we kicked the ball around a bit.

President Clinton was not a bad ballplayer! But, to be honest, my thoughts were in a place way beyond soccer. I was so very happy, and proud of what we'd accomplished. That moment in Mangueira felt like a culmination of things that I'd worked very hard for. My success in soccer had given me a platform to make a difference. My education had given me the skills to do so. The trust that people had put in me, and the hard work my colleagues and I put in at the ministry, resulted in the creation of a project that really did make a positive difference in children's lives. It was a moment to be proud of, for Edson as much as for Pelé.

5

The work with the kids was by far the most rewarding thing I did as minister. We also helped organize soccer tournaments among Brazil's Indians, and games among prisoners in our jails. But there was another group whom I wanted to help as well: soccer players. And while this might not sound at first like a demographic that needed our assistance, given all the other needy folks in Brazil at the time, the truth was that a little government action was long overdue.

Most foreigners assume that Brazilian professional soccer must be thriving. After all, we've got one of the world's richest soccer traditions, a huge base of loyal fans, and a never-ending stream of exciting local talent. So we must have one of the world's best leagues, right? Wrong. Back in the 1990s, the Brazilian league often barely had enough money to pay its players, in part because so many funds were lost to corruption. Nobody really had any idea where all the millions of dollars from tickets and transfer fees went. The stadiums themselves were often unsafe because of rising violence in our society, from which soccer was not immune. As a result, families began staying away from games, and the stands at our big venues—even the Maracanã—were often half empty.

Meanwhile, the rules and regulations—and in some cases, the lack thereof—stripped the players of even their most basic rights. There were no retirement plans, medical help or insurance for Brazilian players. Players also didn't have the right to become "free agents" after their contract with a club was up. If a player couldn't reach a deal with their current team, then their team could forbid them from playing anywhere else. It was almost like human bondage. While a handful of Brazilian stars playing in Europe earned big salaries, most of the players back in Brazil barely got enough money to make a living.

I knew from my travels that Brazil wasn't alone in facing these problems. By the 1990s, soccer leagues in Britain and parts of Europe and the Middle East were also struggling with low attendance. Hooliganism, which some believed sprang from the lawless, rootless culture that took hold in the sixties and seventies, scared off thousands of fans. Meanwhile, the governing bodies that oversaw soccer had perhaps become too powerful. All the money and prestige that entered our beautiful game in the seventies and eighties had suddenly given the presidents and officials at national and global soccer federations a tremendous amount of clout and prestige, but no one had implemented any rules or laws to keep up with the new reality and ensure that they used all this power fairly—and without corruption.

Indeed, for many years, I had been bothered by the way money just seemed to bleed out of soccer. I remembered all those games I played with Santos, all those foreign tours we took to Europe and Africa and the United States, and how the club itself mysteriously never seemed to get any richer. Our training facilities and locker rooms were not top-notch, to say the least. One year, after our usual trip to Europe to play games, a suitcase of money with the team's earnings simply vanished. One of the team officials got off the plane to have a coffee and he said somebody took the suitcase from him. It was like something out of *Mission: Impossible*! Ah, we laugh about it now but these things were actually very sad.

The problem with free agency bothered me so much that I'd been talking to our politicians about it since the early 1970s. I and a group of Santos players flew to Brasilia to meet with President Médici about the issue following an incident on our team. One of our teammates had dated the daughter of one of the team's board members. When they had an argument, the board member insisted the player be removed from the roster—and sure enough, he was fired, and was forbidden from signing with any other teams, either. Labor laws protected virtually every other profession in Brazil from this kind of treatment, but soccer players were treated like third-class citizens.

President Médici seemed sympathetic, but he ended up doing the easy thing: nothing. Now that I was sports minister, I was determined to address the issue. I proposed a whole set of reforms that had the goal of helping both Brazilian players and the teams themselves. Not only would we give players the right to be free agents, but we'd also pass a law obligating soccer clubs to produce annual audited financial reports. This would presumably result in a lot fewer vanished suitcases.

Free agency was clearly an idea whose time had come. But on that second point, regarding financial transparency, I was much less lucky. Virtually every soccer club in the country rebelled against the proposal, because their managers knew it would mean the loss of their special privileges. They even set up a lobby group with an office in Brasilia whose job was to push against the legislation full-time. Meanwhile, there were allegations of corruption at the ministry and I had to fire fourteen people. Every day, there were articles in the press disparaging me for trying to destroy Brazilian soccer, when I was obviously trying to do the opposite.

In 1998, a bill finally did pass—they called it the "Pelé Law." But it was stripped of almost everything but the change to allow free agency, so I'm not even sure in retrospect if it deserves my name.

Getting vilified in the press every day wasn't something I was accustomed to. It was no fun—that's for sure. I was only trying to make soccer as good as it could be. I was trying to make the profession worthy of the game itself. All these years later, it still hasn't happened. Many clubs are struggling with huge debts, and the players are still fighting to earn a good living. Elsewhere in the world, many of the leagues that were in trouble in the 1990s are now doing somewhat better, thanks to better security and more professional management. It's a shame that my country remains stuck in so many ways. Brazilian soccer, and fans of Brazilian soccer, deserve better.

6

Fernando Henrique's successor was Luiz Inácio Lula da Silva, another guy who kind of broke the mold for what Brazilian presidents were supposed to be like. One of twenty-three children born to a man in the northeast, Lula and his family migrated to São Paulo in the back of a truck when he was just a kid. He was the first person from Brazil's working class to become president and, like me, he had done a lot of things with his life despite having very little formal education. He was an inspirational figure to many people not just in Brazil, but around the world.

Lula could be very funny, and very charming. He was a huge soccer fan—and he was elected right after Brazil won its record fifth World Cup, in 2002. But his favorite team was Corinthians, which as I've said, I seemed to always play very well against for some reason. The first couple of times I met Lula, he would laugh and say: "Ahhhhh, Pelé, you son of a gun, how you made me suffer with your damn Santos!" He also asked me to apologize to Dona Celeste on his behalf for cursing her so many times over the years while he watched me play.

We'd laugh and laugh.

I always got along well with Lula. But I was extremely disappointed when I found out, shortly after his election, that he was going to dismantle the *vilas olimpicas*. The *vilas* had been very successful, even after I left the ministry. I pleaded with Lula to reconsider. But he said he wanted to end the program, apparently because his own party had a different project. Not a *better* project, mind you—a different one. And so funding for the *vilas* was cut.

This is one of the things I've never understood about politics. Politicians are so busy fighting one another, and trying to destroy one another's accomplishments for their own self-interest, that they don't think about what's best for the people. The end of the *vilas* was, in my mind, the final proof that politics wasn't the right game for me.

That said, there have been a lot of positive changes in Brazil, and in the world, over the last twenty years or so. Within my own country, some thirty-five million people have been pulled out of poverty and into the middle class—the equivalent of four times the population of New York City. That old Brazilian problem—social and economic inequality—has also improved. Some aspects of the sick, hungry Brazil—the one the team doctors tried to "save" us from prior to the 1958 Cup in Sweden— have faded away. For example, in the 1950s, an average Brazilian could expect to live just forty-six years, compared to sixty-nine years in the United States. That was a huge gap. Today, an average Brazilian can expect to live seventy-three years, just five years behind the U.S. It's no coincidence that, as this improvement took place, we saw school enrollment rise dramatically, thanks in part to the programs that we helped implement during the 1990s. Brazil now has nearly full enrollment at the primary school level. For personal reasons, because of my own past, this gives me enormous satisfaction. It's an achievement that will continue to have benefits for decades to come.

Within Brazil, a lot of people tend to credit our last two presidents for the progress. And it's true: Fernando Henrique and Lula both did a lot of good things. But I've traveled the world enough to know that Brazil does not exist in a vacuum. The same progress we've enjoyed in Brazil has been repeated in countless other countries. Globally, the number of people living in extreme poverty—usually defined as surviving on less than $1.25 a day—has fallen by almost one billion since 1990. I've seen evidence of this on my travels for UNICEF and other organizations to Africa, Southeast Asia, and the rest of Latin America. There is still an enormous amount of poverty in the world, more than there should be. But, with some exceptions, you don't see the same degree of *misery* that you used to. The faces of hunger, disease and hopelessness—the faces I remember seeing often when I was growing up, and in my early travels as a player—are now fewer and farther between.

There are a lot of reasons for the improvement. Even if I understood them perfectly, I wouldn't try to explain them all here. But I think back on my own experiences, and the way the world was back in 1950, when Brazilians gathered as a nation for the first time to listen to the championship game at the Maracanã. After that day, people always seemed more connected to Brazil as a nation, and more likely to think of themselves as part of a community. Once we were unified like that, we could never be pulled fully back apart. In the 1960s, as people became more aware of the world around them, they began demanding greater rights for themselves, and for the poor, in part because they wanted Brazil to be as good in real life as it was on the soccer field. I also think about how, around that same time, we started emphasizing our own individual abilities less and thinking more of teamwork and collaboration. These values were, in turn, becoming more widely accepted around the world, not just on the soccer field.

More recently, as the sport became richer, I've seen again and again how the fruits of soccer's popularity have been used to help the lives of the less fortunate, whether through direct donations or through clinics or other worthwhile programs that enable youths to play organized soccer. Speaking from personal experience—once a boy or a girl steps on a soccer field, they feel equal to everyone else in their village, and in the world. That feeling of pride and empowerment—once kids taste it, it never goes away. They demand more from their politicians. They demand for themselves, and for their families. As well they should.

Yes, I do think soccer has helped make the world a better place. It may not be the main factor—but it has been important. The values that our sport teaches are universal. They've made me a better person, and countless others as well.

7

After all those goals, and all those championships, which do you think is the most famous goal in Brazilian history?

Is it Carlos Alberto's crowning goal in the "Beautiful Team's" final against Italy in 1970?

Didi's rocket that capped "the finest three minutes in soccer" against the Soviet Union in 1958?

Or my header against Sweden in the final minute of that same World Cup?

None of the above. The goal that people still talk about most, that plays over and over in Brazilians' heads, remains Alcides Ghiggia's game-winner against us at the Maracanã in 1950.

It has been sixty-four years! And still . . .

A big part of that goal's enduring hold on us is the fact that Brazil hasn't hosted a World Cup since then. Even though Brazil has won more World Cups than any other country, with five, most of our rivals have enjoyed the pleasure of winning the Cup on their home soil—Argentina, West Germany, England, Italy . . . not us. Believe me, I've seen it: There is nothing quite like celebrating a world championship won in your own country. The patriotism, the mayhem of the crowd, the pride the players feel, is without equal.

Brazil was a finalist to host the Cup in 1994, a bid that I opposed because I believed our country needed to spend its money on other, more important things, as I've already noted. But by the mid-2000s, as the economy improved, it seemed to give us a little breathing room. Meanwhile, Lula's government vowed that not a cent of public money would be spent on World Cup stadiums. He also promised that we'd use the Cup as an excuse to build all kinds of roads and public transportation and airports and other projects that Brazil had been putting off for years, if not decades. So it sounded like a pretty good deal, and I was thrilled when Brazil was awarded the 2014 World Cup. We won the right to host the 2016 Summer Olympics in Rio, and that made me happy and proud as well.

Unfortunately, things haven't turned out as promised. The plan to get private-sector banks to fund the stadiums never really panned out, and public financing was used instead. Many of the big infrastructure projects got canceled or postponed, and the stadiums turned out to be overdue and over budget. I guess I, of all people, should have known better. After all, if you budget one hundred million dollars for a stadium, they *never* build it for ninety million and then say: "Here, you can have the rest of the money back." Especially not in Brazil, and especially not in Brazilian soccer.

By the middle of 2013, a lot of Brazilians were very upset about all of this and staged some street protests during the Confederations Cup, which is a kind of warm-up tournament that takes place a year before the World Cup in the host country. Many people were mad that public financing had been directed to stadiums instead of hospitals and schools and other public services. One Brazilian protester even held up a sign that said: JAPAN, I'D TRADE MY SOCCER FOR YOUR EDUCATION.

As somebody who had once committed the heresy of opposing a World Cup because I didn't think Brazil could afford it, I supported much of what the protesters were saying. There were lots of things to be upset about in Brazil. However, I did worry a bit about politics trickling onto the soccer field itself; I'd seen that happen so many times as a player, and it always made me sad. Some people online were encouraging fans to turn their back on the field during the national anthem, for example. Luckily, the games themselves went ahead as planned. Brazil even ended up winning the Confederations Cup, and all the fans were great about it.

I think that the 2014 World Cup is going to be great fun—a bit of a logistical mess, maybe, but great fun nonetheless. The stadiums will be full of adoring fans, the beaches will be immaculate, and the beverages will be flowing. Brazil knows how to throw a party, and our soccer tradition is second to none. We're known for our hospitality, and our people are eager to welcome the three hundred thousand or so visitors expected. We have some good players on the team, too. I know I'm sure that Brazil, and Brazilian soccer, will win over a whole new generation of fans all over the world.

And if we end up playing Uruguay in the final at the Maracanã, oh my goodness. I might be too nervous to attend. I might have to go to church with Mom instead!

8

I n my office in Santos, I have a picture on my wall of Dondinho, flanked
by me and my son, Edinho. We're each giving him a kiss on the cheek.
It reminds me of some of my happiest days, when Edinho and I would
play soccer in the yard at our house in Guarujá while my dad sat there
and watched. Dad would be quiet for a while. Then he'd start yelling out
tips: "The side of the foot, come on!" And finally, when he just couldn't
take it any longer, he'd get to his feet, smile and say: "Well, boys, pass it
over here! I have a little experience with the ball too, you know!"

Three generations of the Nascimento family, playing soccer and
having a good laugh. Nothing ever made me happier. My dad passed
away in 1997, from heart problems. Soccer hasn't had quite the same
joy for me since. I miss him every day.

When Dondinho died, Mom surprised me by producing an old
relic—my old shoe-shining kit from Baurú. My eyes just about popped
out of my head. I thought that thing had been lost for half a century—I
have no idea where she'd been keeping it. But there it was, with the old
brush and even a little bit of hardened polish still inside. When I opened
it, out popped an old piece of money—a four-hundred-*reis* coin. Brazil has

had seven or eight different currencies in my lifetime, because of all those financial problems we had, and it's impossible to keep track of how much each was worth. But I'm guessing that it would have been a decent bit of change back in the 1950s, especially for a family as poor as ours was.

"What's this?" I asked.

"That's the first money you ever made for us," Mom said softly. "I kept it because you worked so hard for it."

Well, you know me well enough by now to know what I did next! It was a really emotional moment for both of us. It reminded me how fortunate I've been throughout my life. I was blessed by God with a special talent, and lucky enough to be able to use it and enjoy it throughout my entire life. I was able to earn a good living for myself, and support many loved ones as well.

I'm in my eighth decade of life now, and I guess I've started to slow down just a little bit—to set aside a little more time for Edson. When I'm at home in Brazil, in my house just outside Santos, I spend a lot of time in a little garden on the back end of the property. I've got some herbs, some collard greens, and some spring onions and other vegetables. I've been known to lose hours and hours back there, pulling out weeds and watering the plants. It's usually just me and my thoughts; in fact, I jokingly refer to the garden as "my psychologist."

Even there, though, in that quiet, warm patch of lush greenness, the reminders of the life I've lived are ever present. On a trip in the late 1970s to Thailand, I remember tasting a fruit that I found particularly delightful—the lychee, which grows on a tree native to southeast Asia. It's a delicious little thing, a juicy, sweet fruit inside a red, thorny shell. We didn't have lychees in Brazil back then. So—forgive me!—after some deliberation, I decided to smuggle a few seeds back home. I put the seeds inside my shoes. My heart was pounding when I went through customs! But I slipped through undetected, and planted a few of the seeds in my backyard. They're good-sized trees now, and they still produce fruit. During all this time, Brazil and the world have become more open, and you can find lychee in a lot of restaurants and bars in São Paulo and elsewhere. But every time I look at those trees, I remember my travels, and I think about how dramatically the world has changed.

Indeed, the world is never too distant for me. I continue to travel, working for organizations like UNICEF and serving as a global ambassador for the sport. I look after my businesses as well, with the help of Legends 10, the agency that manages my brand and appearances worldwide and develops projects with me to leave a legacy for future generations. Thankfully, many people remain interested in me. I do everything I can to make them happy, especially the kids.

I have a few pet causes I try to look after as well. One of them is the welfare of my teammates from the Brazilian teams of the fifties and sixties. Many of them are in ill health now, broken down physically and struggling to get by financially. I think all of us were heartbroken by what happened to Garrincha, who was very sick and broke near the end of his life. Many of us offered to play in benefit games for him at the Maracanã, or just give him some money, but he always turned it down, saying he was fine. I think that for people who worked their whole lives, and were once on top of the world, it's hard to accept help from friends. So we've worked hard to convince the government to provide something more formal: a little financial help to these older champions, in return for everything they did for Brazil.

I still see a lot of my old teammates from the Brazilian team, and the Santos club. Many of us—Pepe, Zito, Coutinho and I—have been going to the same barber in Santos every two weeks, like clockwork, for the last thirty years. We always have a good laugh. There are two or three restaurants in town where we'll get together every once in a while for somebody's birthday. It's been great to maintain those old friendships. Meanwhile, some of the guys from the 1958 team have, inevitably, begun to pass away. Just last year, in 2013, we lost Djalma Santos, Nilton De Sordi, and Gylmar dos Santos—my beloved teammate whose shoulder I cried on in the wake of our victory against Sweden. Those guys were eighty-four, eighty-two and eighty-three, respectively—they lived good, long lives. Death is a part of life, something that happens to everybody. But I miss those guys nonetheless.

We're trying to put together a Pelé Museum here in Santos. Lots of people have contributed, including the famous Brazilian architect Oscar Niemeyer, who before he died at age 104 was kind enough to make a little sketch of an obelisk that we'll put outside the museum.

My greatest joy comes from family, as it always has. All of my children have made me proud in their own unique way. Kely Cristina lives in New York, and is the mother of four kids. Edinho works as an official for the team at Santos. My daughter Jennifer has a philosophy degree, and does translations. Flavia is a physical therapist, and she helped me recover when I had hip surgery recently. Sandra was a city councilwoman in Santos before she tragically passed away from cancer, leaving behind two children who are now teenagers playing for a local soccer team just outside São Paulo. My two twins from my second marriage, Joshua and Celeste (named after my mother), are teenagers now. Celeste lives and studies with her mom in Florida, while Joshua plays for the Santos youth team. I've told him—just like I've told all my kids—not to worry about trying to follow in my footsteps as a soccer player, or trying to be famous. Every person on this earth, including each of my kids, has his or her own special talent, and place in the world. If that talent allows them to perform in front of the world, and make themselves and other people happy, then that's great. But it doesn't really matter, as long as they discover what their gift is, and they cultivate it.

After all, I've seen firsthand how fleeting fame can be. There's another picture in my office: one of me, seventeen years old, shaking hands with a handsome man in a suit after we won the 1958 Cup. It's hung next to other pictures of me with easily recognizable figures like popes, presidents, and others. Everybody who comes to visit me asks: "Who's that man in the suit?" And it always makes me laugh. That was the king of Sweden, King Gustaf. At that moment, he was the ruler of the nation hosting the Cup, maybe at the center of the world. Barely half a century has passed, and most people don't know who he is anymore. There's a valuable lesson there.

When I look back, it's not the fame or the money that matter most. What I know in my heart is that soccer was good to me, and great to the world. Soccer took a poor kid, gave him a purpose and showed him marvels all around the globe. It led to lifelong friendships, and it created great memories with my family. During my lifetime, I saw how soccer brought people together into communities, and made them more sensitive to the world around them. I saw, time and again, how the sport improved countless millions of lives, both on and off the field. For me, at least, that's why soccer matters.

Acknowledgments

Pelé and Brian Winter would like to thank: Ray Garcia, Jen Schuster and the whole team at Celebra/Penguin for their vision, hard work and support; Paul Kemsley, Chris Flannery, Theresa Tran and everyone at Legends 10; Celso Grellet, José "Pepito" Fornos Rodrigues, Patrícia Franco, Jair Arantes do Nascimento, Andrew Downie, Michael Collett, Ezra Fitz, Jérôme Champagne, Erica Winter, Saul Hudson, Todd Benson, Kieran Murray, Moisés Naím, the Mitchell family, Kenneth Pope, and the Hendee family. In memory of Katherine Winter.

Pelé started his professional career at the age of sixteen for Santos Futebol Clube, a club he stayed with for nearly two decades. In 1958, he won his first World Cup for Brazil at age seventeen—the youngest winner ever. He went on to win another two World Cups in 1962 and 1970, making him the only player in the world today with three Jules Rimet trophies. He is the all-time leading scorer in the history of the sport (1,283 goals in 1,366 matches).

Named one of the "Top 20 Most Important People of the 20th Century" (*Time*) and "Football Player of the Century" (FIFA), Pelé today maintains his commitment to the sport and to society by fulfilling various roles as spokesperson, ambassador and philanthropist.

CONNECT ONLINE
pele10.com
facebook.com/pele
twitter.com/pele

Brian Winter, the chief correspondent for Reuters Brazil, has coauthored several books, including a memoir by Brazil's former president Fernando Henrique Cardoso. He lives in São Paulo.